A Blandford
PET HANDBOOK

Cats

A Blandford
PET HANDBOOK

Cats

Joan Palmer

Blandford Press
POOLE · DORSET

First published in the U.K. 1983 by Blandford Press,
Link House, West Street, Poole, Dorset, BH15 1LL

Copyright © 1983 Blandford Books Ltd

Distributed in the United States by
Sterling Publishing Co., Inc.,
2 Park Avenue, New York, N.Y. 10016

British Library Cataloguing in Publication Data

Palmer, Joan
   Cats.—(A Blandford pet handbook)
   1. Cats
   I. Title
   636.8   SF442

ISBN 0 7137 1204 X

All rights reserved. No part of this book may be
reproduced or transmitted in any form or by any
means, electronic or mechanical, including
photocopying, recording or any information storage
and retrieval system, without permission in writing
from the Publisher.

Typeset by Megaron Typesetting, Boscombe, Bournemouth
Printed in Great Britain by Butler & Tanner Ltd, Frome and London

Contents

	Acknowledgements	6
	Introduction	7
1	Why do you want a cat?	13
2	What you will need	39
3	Feeding	45
4	General care and training	49
5	The show world	53
6	Breeding	65
7	You, your cat and the law	71
8	Health and commonsense care	73
9	Animal cemeteries	81
10	Feline societies	85
	Useful addresses	89
	References	91
	Index	93

Acknowledgements

The author and publisher would like to thank Mr Marc Henrie, who
provided the photographs and the jacket illustration,
Miss Anita Lawrence for the line drawings, and the Pedigree
Education Centre for their assistance in supplying
certain information.

Introduction

If you look at the big cats in their cages at the Zoo you are sure to notice the similarity between them and any pet cat which you may have encountered. This is a natural comparison because the Domestic cat not only looks like a miniature version of its larger relations but also shares a number of characteristics and anatomical features.

All cats have five toes on their fore-paws and four on their hind paws. There is a small pad at the base of each toe and a larger one in the middle of the foot. Cats also have the same balancing ability and what is known as a 'righting reflex', the ability to corkscrew as they fall thereby ending up on all four feet. They have a reflecting layer behind the retina of the eye which becomes more sensitive in dim light, giving them an advantage over other animals in sighting their prey. They also possess a keen sense of smell and, a habit you will come to recognise if you own a cat, the ability to curl up and either 'cat-nap' or sleep contentedly for many hours, exerting themselves only when they are hungry or, in the case of the Domestic cat, when its owner is due home.

Like the Lion, Tiger and other 'big cats', the Domestic cat is a member of the family of carnivorous mammals known as the Felidae. This family is made up of three groups or genera: *Panthera*, the big cats which are able to roar; *Acinonyx*, the Cheetahs, which are exceptional among cats because they cannot retract their claws; and *Felis*, which comprises the remaining cats which cannot roar.

Included in the big cats are: the Lion, Clouded Leopard, Jaguar, Leopard or Panther, Tiger, Snow Leopard and Cheetah. The small cats, which include our friend, the Domestic or pet cat (*Felis catus*),

Above: *Figure 1* The Tiger, one of the largest of the big cats weighing up to 225 kg (495 lb), is nevertheless related to the Domestic cat.

Below: *Figure 2* Geoffroy's cat is one of the smaller wild cats and is found in South America

are: the African Golden cat, Bay cat, Leopard cat or Bengal cat, Chinese Desert cat, Caracal, Jungle cat, Pampas cat, Puma or Mountain Lion, Geoffroy's cat or Ocelot, Kodkod, Iriomote cat, Mountain cat, African Wild cat, Lynx, Pallas's cat, Sand cat, Marbled cat, Black-footed cat, Ocelot, Spanish Lynx, Flat-headed cat, Rusty-spotted cat, Bobcat, Serval, European Wild cat, Temminck's Golden cat, Tiger cat, Fishing cat, Margay or Tree Ocelot and Jaguarundi.

The Domestic cat, which is descended from the African Wild cat, has the same rough tongue and sharp teeth as the big cats. It walks on its toes and can thus creep up stealthily on its prey. It has retractable claws and a supple body, while its paws are cushioned with pads for quiet stalking; its long tail acts as a balancing aid and, in common with the big cats, although it can move very quickly, it cannot keep up a fast pace for long. It chooses instead to wait in ambush for its prey, then creeps up and pounces on its unsuspecting victim. Among cats, the only exception to this method of attack is the Cheetah which chases its prey and can attain a remarkable speed of 100 km/hr (63 mph), which is faster than any other land animal.

The gestation periods of the Wild cat and the Domestic cat are the same and if the Domestic cat were to mate with its wild counterpart, the wild cat looks and temperament would be predominant.

Figure 3 A non-pedigree cat, such as this well-loved tabby, will make an excellent pet

The Domestic cat, moreover, unlike the dog, and despite hundreds of years of domestication, when deprived of home comforts, can revert to the wild and become what is known as a Feral cat, a Domestic cat gone wild, producing young and hunting for food in the wild. The dog, on the other hand, despite its wild ancestry, is unlikely, in most cases, to survive more than 3 weeks relying on its own resources.

Domestication of the cat

How did the cat become domesticated? It is not easy to be factual when there are so many legends concerning the cat. The history of the Domestic cat can certainly be traced back more than 4000 years, at which time it was an esteemed pet in Egyptian homes. There are paintings of cats on the walls of Egyptian tombs and statues and mummified cats have been found in coffins at this time.

The Egyptians, noticing that the pupils of a cat's eyes altered according to the light and that cats were extremely fertile, credited them with magical powers and worshipped them even in the humblest of homes. Their slaughter, if not punishable by death, certainly ensured severe punishment.

At that time, the Egyptians worshipped numerous gods and goddesses with animal-shaped heads. The cat was regarded as sacred to the goddess Isis and became recognised as an incarnation of her. As the daughter of Isis and her husband, Osiris the Sun god, the cat became a goddess in its own right, known as Bast, Bastet or Pasht (the cat-headed goddess). The word 'puss' is said to have been derived from the name 'Pasht'.

Families would mourn passionately for a deceased cat, shaving off their eyebrows and, no doubt, tearing their hair in the traditional manner. As all pet cats were carefully guarded, it is a wonder that any found their way from Egypt to other parts of the world.

Gradually cat-worship waned and, although the creature was still held in some esteem, it became valued for its more practical abilities, such as rodent-killing. The cat was probably introduced into northern Europe by traders in the time of Christ and reached Britain by the first or second century A.D., in company with the Romans. This is borne out by footprints found in clay tiles and by bones found in the remains of Roman villas.

The cat must have had a difficult time in Britain in the Middle Ages. On one hand, it was feared and disliked because of its believed association with black magic—this was at a time when harmless men and women could be put to death merely for owning a cat, particularly a *black* one, which was interpreted as being a 'familiar'. On the other hand, its value in keeping down rodents was immense, for Britain was fighting the plague which had spread into Europe from Asia. The plague was eventually to wipe out half the population of London before being brought under control by the Great Fire in 1666.

However, by the time Queen Victoria came to the British throne, the cat had found a new respectability. It was thought of by the morally conscious Victorians as a creature not only of beauty, but of exceptional cleanliness, as well as representing the epitome of good motherhood. So, while it was not exactly worshipped as in Egyptian times, the cat certainly was depicted on innumerable postcards, cushions, chocolate boxes and samplers, many of which have now become collectors' pieces.

The cat, indeed, had such a strong association with Britain that, when it was introduced to the American colonies to control an invasion of rats, the people there began to refer to the rat as the 'Hanover rat', associating it with the House to which British royalty in those days belonged.

Characteristics of the cat

What is there of the cat's character that we have not learned already? Cats, like all creatures, are individuals and it is sad that so many people categorise each animal as automatically having the traits attributed to cats as a whole.

Generally, the Domestic cat has a gentle, docile nature and, although many will declare that its fondness is of its home and familiar surroundings rather than of those who own it, there have been many examples of cats walking incredible distances to rejoin their owners and of cats who have survived innumerable moves, without ill effect, in order to remain with their favourite people. Of course, there are bad-tempered cats just as there are bad-tempered people, but usually it is found that such cats have been teased or ill-treated.

Again, despite the oft-heard assumption that cats and dogs fight, it is a familiar sight to see a cat and dog curled up in one basket or eating out of the same dish, although obviously such rapport is best achieved when the pets have been brought up together from a few months of age.

That a cat is independent cannot be disputed and, having a good share of intelligence, who can blame it if, in the event of its food and creature comforts not being provided, it takes itself to more congenial lodgings.

When cared for correctly, however, the cat can show unmistakable affection both for its owners and other family pets, and it will turn up regularly at meal times, spend hours (especially in winter) in front of the fireside and, in many cases, be waiting for you on the doorstep, or rush down the road to meet you if you return at a regular time every day.

1
Why do you want a cat?

Why do you want to own a cat? Maybe there was always a cat in your childhood home and you feel that a house is not a home without a cat in it. Perhaps you just want an undemanding pet. You may have become acquainted with one or more of the exotic pure-bred cat varieties and are excited not only by the prospect of owning such a beautiful creature, but also by the thought of becoming actively involved in the Cat Fancy and exhibiting your cat in shows and, possibly, breeding kittens of your own.

You may have acquired a cat already and bought this book merely to learn more about your pet and how to give it the best possible care. What we want to find out now, however, is whether you will prove to be a suitable owner and should be entrusted with a delightful, knowing creature whose demands are comparatively few. The very fact that a cat is undemanding is probably why it is often acquired somewhat casually. Alas, it may also be relinquished equally casually when its owners are moving, divorcing, going abroad, or their circumstances otherwise change, making it inconvenient to keep a full-grown cat, whose antics as a kitten formerly delighted them.

Would you make a suitable owner?

The cat, unlike a dog, does not need to be taken out for walks so there is no need for the owner to take unwanted exercise, or even to get out of bed early and open the door to the garden, for this pet can let itself in and out by means of an open window or, better still, by a cat flap which renders the home much less vulnerable to burglars.

Nor does ownership of a cat preclude you from taking a full-time job as it would with a dog. The essentials are shelter, a means of access to the house (which means a cat flap) and somebody who will feed it every day. Although these are the basic needs, they are by no means all that knowledgeable pet-owners would wish to offer their cat and it would be most unfair were you to buy a cat with only these essentials in mind.

A cat may be able to survive given just the crude necessities of life, but if it is to lead a healthy contented life and, at the same time, to develop a lifelong rapport with its owner, the most essential ingredient is love and, despite its reputation for indifference, the cat, given care and attention, will return this a hundredfold.

The cat enjoys a settled routine with regular meals and the company of its owner whenever possible. Love and affection is an essential ingredient for keeping a cat or, indeed any pet animal. Part of the fascination of keeping a pet is to observe the development of its character and personality.

Is your accommodation suitable?

The ideal home for a cat, one imagines, must be a rambling country farmhouse with a warm kitchen and acres of garden set well away from threatening traffic. There are, however, many cats living long, blissfully happy lives in anything from a one-roomed apartment in London or New York to a semi-detached or terraced house with little more than a patch of lawn and a tree on which it can climb and sharpen its claws.

Luckily, the cat will adapt to almost any surroundings, regardless of its owner's wealth or location, but if, for instance, it is to live in town or in an upstairs apartment, its owner will need to supply certain accessories and facilities to compensate for those which would normally be available in a more rural setting (see Chapter 2).

Wherever you live, do not believe the old story that you ought to put a cat out for the night. The place for your cat at night is in your home, not prowling out of doors, although you should always encourage it to go out and relieve itself before you go to bed.

Choosing a pedigree cat

If you have already set your heart on a Seal-point Siamese, a Cornish Rex or a glamorous Russian Blue, I wish you every joy. On the other

WHY DO YOU WANT A CAT?   15

hand, if you are a newcomer to the world of cats and would like to know something of the choice that is open to you, the following information should help.

Basically, a pedigree cat belongs to a variety for which a standard has been laid down by a governing body, e.g. the Governing Council of the Cat Fancy in the UK, or the Cat Fanciers Association Inc. in the USA, and whose forebears have been similarly registered for at least four generations. There is often some confusion over the British term 'pedigree' as applied to cats or dogs. The Americans prefer to use the term 'pure-bred' which, in fact, seems more correct, as a Certificate of Pedigree is what is given to the buyer of a pure-bred animal.

One of the best ways of seeing some of the eighty or more breeds for which a show standard exists is by attending a cat show, such as the National Cat Club Show at Olympia in London or the Empire Cat Club Show in New York. Not only is there the largest variety of breeds at these big shows but the animals on display are amongst the very best examples of their breeds.

Figure 4 Bicolour Long-hair

Common varieties of cat

Every cat for which there is a standard has an official breed number. Cats can be grouped into Long-haired, Short-haired and Siamese but are usually divided into two main sections, those with long hair whose ancestors came from Ankara (Angora) in Turkey and Persia, and those with short hair. Cats with short coats are sub-divided into:

a) those with short hair, round heads, big rounded eyes and shortish thick tails known as British cats (said to be descended from cats that came with the Romans),
b) foreign Short-hairs with longish heads, almond-shaped eyes and long thin tails which originated from the Far East,
c) Siamese or similar shape but with pale fur on the bodies and dark faces, ears, legs and tail,
d) the Rex, which are slim cats with unusual very short curly fur.

Figure 5 British Short-hair: Silver Tabby

WHY DO YOU WANT A CAT? 17

To complicate matters still further, in the USA, long-haired cats whose ancestors came from Persia and other places, are still referred to as 'Persians'; this means that the American classification groups all long-haired cats, except Angora, Balinese, Birman, Himalayan and Turkish Van cats, as Persians.

Whatever the complexities of classification, there is no doubt that there are some very beautiful cats available.

Figure 6 A blue-eyed Foreign White with long thin tail and almond-shaped eyes

Cat varieties and breed numbers

Long-haired cats

1	Black	7	Silver Tabby
2	Blue-eyed White	8	Brown Tabby
2a	Orange-eyed White	9	Red Tabby
2b	Odd-eyed White	10	Chinchilla
3	Blue	11	Tortoiseshell
4	Red Self	12	Tortoiseshell and White
5	Cream	12a	Bi-coloured
6	Smoke	13	Blue Cream
6a	Blue Smoke	13a	Any Other Colour

13b	(1) Seal Colour-point		20	Brown Tabby
	(2) Blue Colour-point		21	Tortoiseshell
	(3) Chocolate Colour-point		22	Tortoiseshell and White
	(4) Lilac Colour-point		25	Manx
	(5) Red Colour-point		25a	Stumpie Manx
	(6) Tortie Colour-point		25b	Tailed Manx
	(7) Cream Colour-point		26	Any Other Variety
	(8) Blue-Cream Colour-point		28	Blue-Cream
	(9) Chocolate-Cream Colour-point		30	Spotted
			31	Bi-coloured
	(10) Lilac-Cream Colour-point		36	Smoke
13c	Birman		39	British Shorthair Tipped
13d	Turkish			
50b	Self Chocolate			
50c	Self Lilac			

Foreign short-haired cats

16a	Russian Blue
23	Abyssinian
23a	Sorrel Abyssinian
23c	Blue Abyssinian
27	Burmese (Brown)
27a	Blue Burmese
27b	Chocolate Burmese
27c	Lilac Burmese
27d	Red Burmese
27e	Tortie Burmese
27f	Cream Burmese
27g	Blue Tortie Burmese
27h	Chocolate Tortie Burmese
27j	Lilac Tortie Burmese
29	Havana
29c	Foreign Lilac
33	Cornish Rex
33a	Devon Rex
34	Korat
35	Foreign White
37	Foreign Black
37a	Foreign Blue
38	Oriental Spotted Tabby
38a	Blue Oriental Spotted Tabby
38b	Chocolate Oriental Spotted Tabby
38c	Lilac Oriental Spotted Tabby
38d	Red Oriental Spotted Tabby
38f	Red Oriental Spotted Tabby

51	(1) Red Shell Cameo
	(2) Red Shaded Cameo
	(3) Red Smoke Cameo
	(4) Red Tortie Cameo
52	(1) Cream Shell Cameo
	(2) Cream Shaded Cameo
	(3) Cream Smoke Cameo
	(4) Blue-Cream Cameo

Siamese cats

24	Seal-Point Siamese
24a	Blue-Point Siamese
24b	Chocolate-Point Siamese
24c	Lilac-Point Siamese
32	Tabby-Point Siamese
32a	Red-Point Siamese
32b	Tortie-Point Siamese
32c	Cream-Point Siamese
32x	Any Other Colour Siamese

Short-haired cats

14	Blue-eyed White
14a	Orange-eyed White
14b	Odd-eyed White
15	Black
16	British Blue
17	Cream
18	Silver Tabby
19	Red Tabby

There are a number of unusual cats which do not appear in this table either because there is no standard for them at the time of writing or because they have been placed on an experimental register, with a draft standard, prior to an official breed number being allocated.

It will be appreciated that more breeds are constantly being developed for which official recognition is sought, but that these cannot be given status until a sufficient number of specimens have been bred to an acceptable and recognisable standard.

In a book of this size, it would be impossible to deal in detail with all the cats mentioned, so I will confine myself to some of the best loved and unusual in the hope that this will encourage you sufficiently to see some of them for yourself.

Siamese cats

The best known pedigree variety is probably the Siamese with its unmistakable bright blue, almond-shaped eyes, wedge-shaped head, long nose and distinctive call. It is an interesting fact, as I have proved for myself, that a cross-bred kitten brought up with a Siamese will learn to vocalise in just the same way.

The Siamese is distinguishable also by its points—the dark patches on a body of pale cream fur. These points appear on the face, ears, paws and tail. The most common are the dark points of the Seal-point followed by those of the Blue-point and the Lilac-point. The latter was developed in the USA in the 1930s and the points are a delicate lilac-grey. There is also the Chocolate-point, whose points are an irresistible milky chocolate. All Siamese kittens are white when born and the points develop later.

It is said that the Siamese graced the Royal Palace in Bangkok, Thailand, almost 100 years ago. Another theory, put forward by Siamese expert, May Dunnill, as to the origin of the Siamese cat, is that it may be a descendant of a cat seen in the 1700s in the region of the Caspian Sea by Peter Simon Pallas, a German explorer and naturalist. This cat is reported to have been the offspring of a black cat and had a light chestnut-brown body colour, black at the back and paler along the sides and belly, with a black streak running along and surrounding the eyes, ending at the front of the forehead. The ears, paws and tail were black and its head was longer towards the nose than that of the common cat. Mrs Dunnill has also spoken of a picture in Pallas's book showing a cat with a Siamese coat pattern.

Being a Siamese cat owner myself, gives me the opportunity of defending the breed's undeserved reputation for destructiveness. I am prepared to believe that some members of this breed do tear wallpaper and rip chair covers, but I have never known of one and nor have the owners whom I have encountered. I have to agree that the Siamese has a strong, determined personality and, for this reason alone, a lonely person wanting a strong character with which to communicate could not chose a better companion. The Siamese enjoys the sound of its own voice immensely and has a number of distinctive calls with which it expresses its needs and reactions. Moreover, it can be relied on to answer back!

Figure 7 *Chocolate Point Siamese*

WHY DO YOU WANT A CAT?

Very often a person who really wanted a dog but was unable to keep one has found a Siamese cat to be equally satisfactory as a companion. A Siamese, encouraged from kittenhood, will not only follow its owner around and hold a conversation, but can also be taken out for walks on a lead.

The Siamese can be very shy when a kitten and, until you win its confidence, there can be moments of despair while you search every nook and cranny to find its latest hiding place. Persevere with loving kindness, however, and you will have a feline friend unsurpassed.

Although I have mentioned that the Seal-point, Lilac-point, Blue-point and Chocolate-point cats are most popular, it might be advisable to see some of the other colours which have been developed, such as the Red-point Siamese, with its red golden points, or the Tortoiseshell-point which is very distinctive, before deciding on a purchase. If the characteristics of the Siamese cat appeal to you but you prefer long-haired cats, there is now the exquisite Balinese, which has long, very soft silky hair. The Balinese is a pure-bred Siamese, developed from a Persian/Siamese crossing.

Figure 8 Blue Point Balinese

The Burmese cat

Also much loved and a delight to the eye, is the Burmese cat, particularly, in my opinion, the Brown Burmese, a colour referred to as sable in the USA.

The coat of the Brown Burmese shades slightly from a rich, dark seal-brown on the top of the back to a slightly lighter colour underneath. There is also a slight intensification of colour as they grow older. When they begin life, they are an enchanting coffee colour which gradually darkens until, between the ages of 9 and 24 months, they achieve their true coat colour. A healthy Burmese has a fine, silky, close-lying coat with a characteristic natural sheen. The cats are medium-sized, strong and muscular. Other distinctive features are a short, blunt, wedge-shaped face, with a short muzzle showing no jaw pinch. The ears are erect and wide at the base, with the opening well to the front and the top of the skull is nicely rounded between the ears. The eyes are large and expressive, ranging in colour from chartreuse-yellow to golden yellow. In common with the Siamese, the tail tapers only slightly to a rounded tip.

The Burmese is extremely friendly, affectionate, active and playful and in my experience, those people who have owned this variety consider no other when it comes to replacing a much-loved pet.

Figure 9 Blue Burmese: Ch. *Sabra Blue Poppy*

Rex cats

One's first glimpse of a Rex cat is always memorable for, rather like the Hairless cat, which to some represents beauty and others an aberration, the Rex, with its wavy coat which makes it look for all the world as if it had been rescued from the bath tub, is indeed an intriguing and desirable variety.

There are, in fact, two types of Rex which are easily confused as they differ only slightly in the shape of their heads and the thickness of their fur. These are the Cornish Rex and the Devon Rex; both have wedge-shaped heads, long ears and long bodies with whip-like tails.

The Cornish Rex is the original Rex mutation, first discovered in Cornwall in 1950. These early Rex were outcrossed to British shorthairs but, since 1965, breeders have aimed for foreign type. The Cornish Rex resembles the sacred cat of ancient Egypt, but the coat forms waves over the body. The head, body, legs and tail are proportionally long.

Figure 10 Blue Smoke Cornish Rex

The Devon Rex, the second Rex mutation, did not appear until 1960. Matings to Cornish females produced straight-coated offspring, which proved the two mutations to be dissimilar. This mutation was perpetuated by back-crossing the first filial generation to the sire. The Devon Rex coat is closely waved, the type is foreign, but the head is full-cheeked with a whisker break. The Devon has a rather pixy-like face. The nose of the Cornish Rex is more Roman. Both these cats are most affectionate and extremely cheeky and playful. I find them totally irresistible. The curly coat of the Cornish Rex is very similar to that of the Astrex rabbit.

Figure 11 White Devon Rex

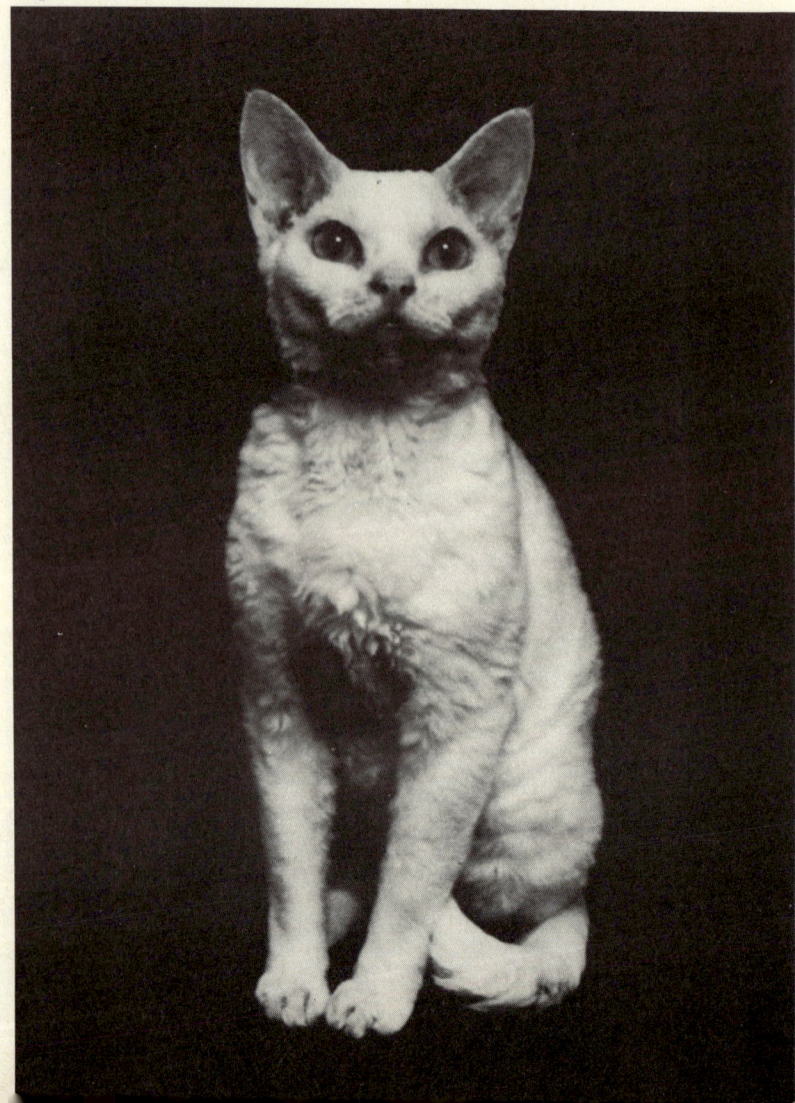

The Russian Blue cat

The Russian Blue is a very lovely cat which, until the late 1940s, was known as the Archangel Blue because it is thought to have come from Archangel, a Baltic port. The first imports into the UK were Lingpopo and Iula, both of which came from Archangel and were owned by Mrs Carew-Cox of Saffron Walden, Essex. Other names by which this variety has been known include the Blue Foreign, the Spanish and the Maltese. This cat is noted for its short, thick silvery blue coat, which is like seal-skin in texture, and its dainty build. The head of the Russian Blue is small, the eyes are green and the ears are large and vertical. They are very silent, sweet-natured cats.

Figure 12 Russian Blue queen with kittens

When the Russian Blue was introduced into the UK towards the end of the nineteenth century it was, at times, confused with the native short-haired British Blue and one found specimens of both breeds being exhibited in one and the same class, despite the differences of body type and head structure—the Russian Blue having a much longer head. The breeds, however, soon became separate and the Russian, for a while, was known as the Blue Foreign, a state of affairs which existed until the end of World War 2, when interest in breeding the Russian Blue was renewed. In the mid-1960s, the breed standard was revised and the Russian Blue was given its own exclusive show standards in both the UK and the USA.

It is not a good idea to keep two Russian Blue toms as they may fight.

The Abyssinian cat
This attractive variety is said to resemble the cats of ancient Egypt. Murals and statues of that time illustrate cats of this shape. The type is foreign, with a long body, long pointed head, sharp ears and a fairly long, tapered tail.

The Abyssinian differs from all other short-hairs in the unique coat of ruddy brown with black or brown tickings. There should be no bars

Figure 13 Lilac Abyssinian

or other markings. The chin should not be white, but it is difficult to breed out this defect. It is also possible to produce red-coated and blue-coated Abyssinians and these colours are recognised by the Abyssinian Cat Club.

The Abyssinian was first recognised in the UK in 1882 but does not appear to have been exhibited until the 1930s. It has, however, made up for lost time being among the three highest pure-bred cat registrations (after the Siamese and Burmese) in the USA.

The Abyssinian is a friendly cat which likes nothing better than to be with its owner, fulfilling ideally the role of exhibition cat and fireside companion.

The Korat cat

The Korat always draws a crowd of admirers at cat shows, particularly because of its unique, heart-shaped face. This comparative newcomer, with its small head, large vivid green eyes and silver-blue body, found its way to the UK from the USA and has only been

Figure 14 Korat

exhibited since the 1960s. However, its existence can be traced back in history to its native Thailand where it is called the *si-sawat*, a Thai word, the translation of which means 'mixture of grey and pale green heralding good luck', a fact which has given the Korat the reputation of being a lucky cat. It is depicted as such in a volume of illustrations which can be seen today in the National Museum of Bangkok.

The Korat is a sweet-natured, intelligent animal with the oriental trick of regarding its owners as its servants, in a manner rather similar to that of the Siamese. A word of warning—refrain from choosing this variety if your living conditions are somewhat cold, because this cat is subject to respiratory trouble and should ideally be kept in a centrally-heated home.

The Havana cat

The Havana cat is a dainty, fine-boned cat with a coat of rich chestnut-brown showing no ghost points. The type is foreign with a long, wedge-shaped head, large ears and a long tapering tail. The eyes should be almond-shaped and green in colour. The legs are slim with dainty oval paws and pink footpads. The colour is exactly the same as that of the Chocolate-point Siamese and this cat is best described as Self Chocolate.

Figure 15 Havana

The Havana's body is similar to that of the Siamese, but its rich brown coat is very different from that of the Burmese. Kittens are born with the same coat colour as the adult.

Unlike the Korat, this is a hardy, fun cat, well able to stand up to the elements. It is a popular show cat and, like the Abyssinian, will probably combine the role of pet and exhibit admirably. There is some slight difference in the desired standard of this cat in the USA and UK, the Americans preferring oval eyes rather than the oriental eyes favoured in this country.

The Black cat
In the Middle Ages, the Black cat was thought to be a portent of evil and the instrument of Satan. Nowadays it is an omen of good luck and we believe that good fortune will befall us if a self-coloured Black cat crosses our path. Short-haired Black cats are more frequently seen than long-haired ones.

The broad-headed Long-haired Black, with its blazing orange eyes and sinister look, might well have been considered the instrument of supernatural powers in the past. Nowadays, however, it is more likely to be a much sought-after pet.

Figure 16 Black Long-hair

The Chinchilla cat

The Chinchilla is the glamour puss of the cat world; its pure white fur tipped with black gives it a fairy-tale look.

The head of the Chinchilla is broad with small ears and eyes of a beautiful sea-green colour. The kittens are dark at birth and it is hard to credit that they will become such beauties. They make delightful pets but do remember that their long coats must be groomed every day. Despite its glamorous appearance and need for attention, the Chinchilla is a robust cat and should not present its owner with any problems.

Figure 17 White Chinchilla

Angora cats

Mention of an Angora cat usually brings to mind a beautiful longhaired white cat. However, although the Angora is being bred again in the UK, you are more likely to see a delectable Chocolate Angora or one of some other colour and pattern.

The ancestors of cats with long hair came from Ankara (Angora) in Turkey and also from Persia. However, it was the Persian type that became most popular and, as a result, the Angora slowly dropped out of the Fancier's scene. Now, however, interest has been revived and, while the British are producing a variety of Angora in a range of

Figure 18 Chocolate Angora

colours, the Americans are developing a variety which they call the Turkish Angora. This cat has a wedge-shaped head, a long supple body and long thin tail. The ears are large and its fur is not as long as that of most other long-hairs.

The White Long-haired cat

This is a really gorgeous cat with a beautiful, long, pure white coat and good tail. The head is broad and round, the ears small and its large eyes are deep orange in colour. Sometimes, however, Whites have blue eyes or even one orange eye and one blue eye. The variety occurs in three types known as the Blue-eyed White, the Orange-eyed White and the Odd-eyed White and, while the Odd-eyed variety is not everyone's idea of beauty, it is certainly a strange experience to behold this beautiful long-coated white cat, boasting one superb blue eye and the other a perfect orange. It is necessary, however, when choosing a cat of this type, to make absolutely certain that it is not deaf on the blue-eyed side. This variety is undoubtedly descended from the Angoran cats, which were brought from Turkey to the UK *via* France, so that, for a time, they were also known as French cats.

Figure 19 Odd-eyed White Long-hair

It was thought in the early days that White Long-hairs were cold, unresponsive little creatures until it was found that they could not hear. However, cross-breeding has now almost eliminated this disability but care should be taken.

The Birman cat

The Birman, unlike the Burmese, is long-haired. It is a descendant of the temple cats in Burma, whose white socks and colouring can be traced back to before the birth of Christ.

The Birman has a superb nature—gentle, loving, with a quiet voice. It walks with a tiger-like gait, has deep, blue eyes, points like the Siamese and four white feet. On the back legs, there is a gauntlet-like spur, reaching to the first joint.

There are Blue-point Birmans and also Seal-point Birmans. In the Seal-point, the body fur is a clear pale beige, slightly golden with dark brown points and, in the Blue-point, the body fur is bluish white, rather cold in tone with blue-grey points. Chocolate-point Birmans and Lilac-point Birmans are also beginning to appear. The Birman has a longer body than most long-hairs and its head is not so broad.

Figure 20 Three generations of Seal Point Birmans

The Manx cat

The Manx cat, although out of the ordinary, cannot truthfully be categorised as rare for it is well known in the UK and the USA.

The Manx differs from all other varieties in having no tail and there should be a slight hollow where the tail should start. The head is round and large, with a longish nose and full cheeks, the ears being a little pointed. The fur is short and soft and may be of any colour. Because of its hoppity walk, this variety was once known as the 'rabbit cat'.

A Manx litter may contain kittens without tails and kittens with very short tails known as 'stumpies'. It is not always easy to bring them up successfully and very careful weaning is necessary. The rump of the Manx is expected to be as round as an orange. The Manx, which is still bred in the Isle of Man where it originated, was particularly popular in the nineteenth century in the UK, since when its popularity has fluctuated. It is popular in the USA on the show benches where it is a frequent prizewinner. Incidentally, the breed's lack of tail does not seem to preclude it from balancing in the same way as other cats when climbing. It has an equable nature and is pleasant and rewarding to keep.

Figure 21 Black Manx

Unusual varieties of cat

The Japanese Bobtail
This is an ancient Japanese variety which is quite unique. Its tail is 4-5 in (10-12 cm) in length and curled so that it tends to look much shorter. Its back legs, which are long and generally bent, give the back a level appearance. The Japanese Bobtail is tri-coloured, red, white and black, although some other colours are accepted in the USA. This cat is said to shed less of its hair than other varieties.

It is not as yet bred in the UK but has caught on as an exhibit in the USA. One hopes that it will soon appear in the UK. After all, the mere acquisition of such a cat is regarded as lucky, while, in Japan, to be given one is regarded as a measure of great esteem.

The Bobtail has an equable temperament but is somewhat aloof and has a characteristic in common with certain toy breeds of dog in that it recognises and enjoys the company of its own kind. The female is reluctant to part company with her kittens, preferring, if possible, to live in a family unit.

The Scottish Fold cat
This mutation has the disapproval of a number of breed authorities. It has drop ears and was developed from a kitten of this type born in Scotland. One description of the Scottish Fold likened it to a Tabby cat with the ears of a Boxer dog—not with ears cropped in Continental style, of course!

The Peke-Faced Persian cat
This is a long-haired breed, recognised only in the USA, which has been developed from Red Self and Tabby Long-hairs with heavy jowls. It is unusual in that the nose resembles that of a Pekingese dog. However, as it suffers from breathing problems and trouble with tear ducts, troubles which, indeed, are encountered by the Pekingese dog, there is some controversy as to whether this type should be perpetuated.

The Sphynx
The Sphynx is a hairless cat which is recognised in the USA and Canada and, probably because there is a similar breed of dog—the Mexican Hairless—in some references it is referred to as the Mexican Hairless cat. (It would, however, be more correctly named the

Canadian Hairless as it was a mutation which occurred there in 1966, the offspring, as far as one can gather, of short-haired domestic cats. The hairless kitten was mated with its dam [i.e. back-crossed], resulting in more hairless kittens. Mating between hairless cats did not produce further hairless cats and it was only when the hairless cat was out-crossed and bred with American short-hairs that it reproduced itself.)

The Sphynx is a most regal animal, with no coat except for a little pile on the face, which feels just like velvet, and some hair on the testicles. Unlike the Mexican Hairless dog, however, which has a high body temperature, the hairless cat cannot bear the cold, so central heating is essential if you wish to keep one, although no other special attention is required.

The Feral cat
Finally, passing over such rarities as the Ragdoll, a mutation developed in California from a Persian queen whose kittens seemed impervious to pain or danger, the European Wild cat, seen sometimes in the highlands of Scotland, and the Maine Coon cat, which probably evolved through crossings between the short-haired cats of settlers and Angoras brought by sailors from the east, we arrive at the Feral cat. The Feral cat is a Domestic cat turned wild or the offspring of an unwanted pet which has been reared in the wild.

Feral cats can be distinguished from the true Wild cat by the pointed tail-tip and smaller head. Domestic cats are able to fend for themselves if necessary and will survive and breed in the wild. Perhaps the most remarkable feature, however, is that, after several generations, cats of this type revert to a Tabby coat pattern.

Buying a cat

Before you set out to buy or acquire a cat, do make sure, in the case of a pure-bred, especially if you are answering an advertisement, that you know exactly what you are going to see and that you have not committed yourself to making a purchase.

Most people have a preference for either long-coated or short-coated animals, so if you have not done your homework properly it is obviously going to be a disappointment if you answer an advertisement for a Persian type when you really want a cat with a short coat, such as a Siamese or Burmese. There are other considerations to bear in mind. If you are houseproud, for instance, long white hairs will show up on the carpet, whereas the hairs of a short-coated breed may go almost undetected.

I have talked mainly about cats of pure breeding but perhaps you are not seeking a pedigree cat at all but simply have a loving home to offer an available kitten or cat. If this is the case, you should have little difficulty. You may know someone whose queen has recently had kittens, answer an advertisement in your local newspaper or just see what you want in the pet-shop window.

If you do have difficulty in finding a kitten, there are many organisations which you can contact, such as the Royal Society for the Prevention of Cruelty to Animals, the People's Dispensary for Sick Animals and the Cats Protection League (in the UK) and the American Society for the Prevention of Cruelty to Animals, the Animal Protection Institute of America and the Bide-a-Wee Association (in the USA). Addresses for these and other societies are given at the end of this book.

Several of these organisations have local branches and inspectors whom you will be able to contact and, while in some cases a small charge for a kitten or cat will be made, in others you may find that there is no charge at all, or that you are asked to make a donation of as much as you feel you can afford or, indeed, feel that the service is worth.

Do not be indignant if, about a month after you get your cat, you receive a visit from a home-checker. Certainly you will do so if you obtain a cat from the RSPCA. This is to ensure that the pet has settled in happily and to assist you with any problems you may have. The home-checker is not trying to catch you out, merely to help you and your pet have a happy life together.

In some cases you may be asked to sign a form agreeing that, if at any time you cannot keep the cat, it will be returned to the care of the Society. It may also be stipulated that the cat should be neutered (male) or spayed (female) when it reaches 4 or 5 months of age or that a grown cat should be similarly doctored if this has not already been done.

Such a course may well be considered unnatural but many thousands of cats and kittens are destroyed each year because there are just not enough homes to go round. Moreover, a queen can have up to three litters of three to four kittens annually from the age of about 5 months so it must be considered a kindness and not a cruelty to take this course of action.

Do not think that only cross-bred cats are available from rescue societies. In fact, although the majority of such animals are of mixed breeding, it is not unknown for a Siamese or other type of pure-bred cat to be needing a home, perhaps where the owners have gone abroad or a breeder has had to reduce the numbers in a cattery.

The normal procedure when seeking a cat aristocrat however, is to locate a responsible breeder of the variety in which you are interested. You can do this by writing (enclosing a stamped addressed envelope) either, in the UK, to the Secretary of the Governing Council of the Cat Fancy or, in the USA, to the Cat Fanciers Association Inc. or the Cat Fanciers Federation Inc. These organisations can supply names and addresses of breeders and give you the addresses of specialist cat clubs and societies. It is likely that they will also be able to give the dates of important cat shows. Attendance at these provides an excellent opportunity to see all the pure-bred varieties under one roof and talk to the breeders and exhibitors. Cats and kittens are often offered for sale at such shows. Two of the most important are the National Cat Club Show, held annually at Olympia in London, either in November or December, and the Empire Cat Club Show, which is held at Madison Square Gardens in New York, in February or March, under the auspices of the Cat Fanciers Federation.

Most exhibitors will be delighted to show you their cats and the only problems you are likely to encounter are which cat to choose and how to restrict yourself to just one.

2
What you will need

The basic essentials for keeping a cat, if there is access to a garden, are minimal; a cosy basket and dishes for food and drink will suffice. If no garden is available, it is advisable, before acquiring your cat, to grow some grass in a window-box or flower-pot. Cats need to eat grass, which is a natural medicine, relieving bile and acting as an emetic. Cats are also particularly fond of coltsfoot.

Sleeping quarters

If you are bringing up a kitten and a puppy together they will probably develop a firm friendship and want to share each other's body warmth in a basket. Otherwise, cats welcome their own basket or raised box, placed in a draught-free position which, in winter, should be close to a fire or stove.

There are many ornate and novel cat baskets from which to choose,

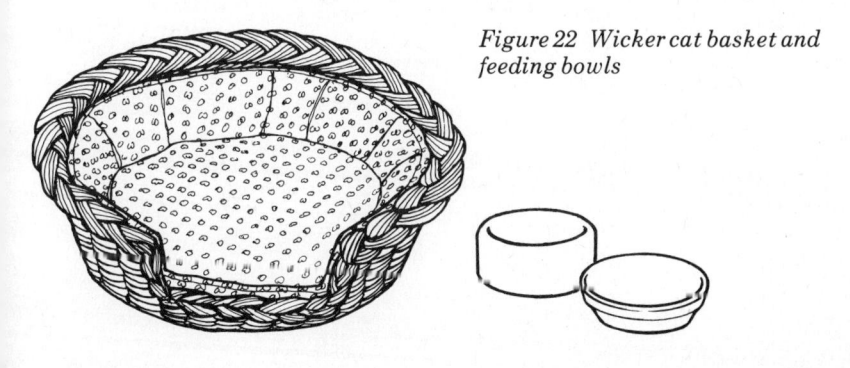

Figure 22 Wicker cat basket and feeding bowls

including the 'Cat Igloo', with a beehive-type roof, made of washable plastic and smart enough to grace the grandest of living rooms. Plastic or wicker baskets are my personal preference as they are very easily cleaned and, therefore, do not harbour germs. They should be washed regularly in a dilute solution of disinfectant.

On the market, there are some first-class, synthetic sheepskin materials, purpose-made for animal bedding and able to stand up to a great deal of wear and tear and frequent washing. 'Vet-bed' is one such material. Such a bed-lining, supplemented if you wish with old sweaters, cardigans or cushions, will ensure that your pet has a comfortable resting-place.

If you have acquired a kitten and feel that the heat in your kitchen may not be sufficiently constant to give the warmth that it needs, you can obtain a pet-bed warmer from a pet-shop. This consists of a slim metal panel which can be placed under the bedding and plugged by a lead attachment into an electric power point. It is, of course, thermostatically controlled. Alternatively you can put a rubber hot-water bottle, wrapped in an old sweater or blanket in the kitten's basket.

Scratching posts

A scratching post is also recommended to deter your pet from scratching the furniture. A number of styles are available, ranging from a simple piece of cork bark, treated with a tempting cat lick, to elaborate and not always inexpensive furnishing arrangements.

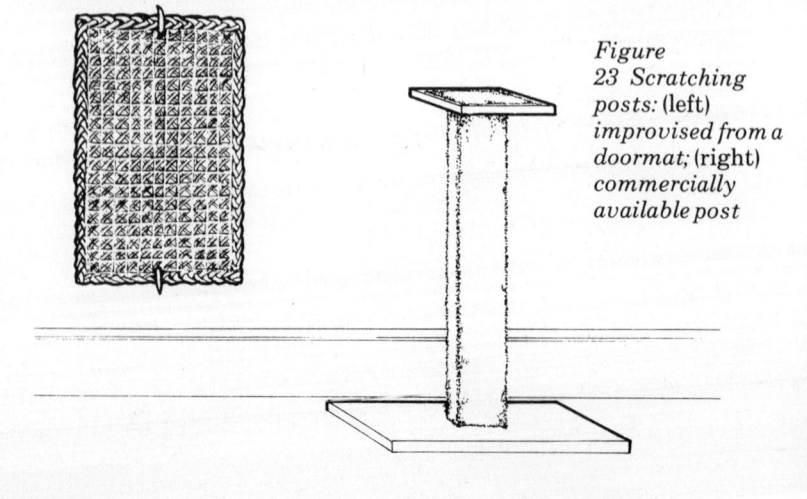

Figure 23 Scratching posts: (left) improvised from a doormat; (right) commercially available post

Cat flaps

I consider a cat flap to be one of the most important purchases of all. Its installation involves only simple carpentry and afterwards your cat will be able to enter and leave the house as it wishes.

Figure 24 Cat flap: (left) *front view;* (right) *side view showing mode of operation*

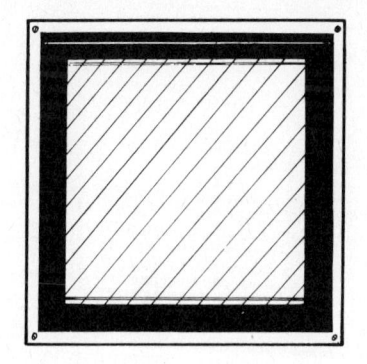

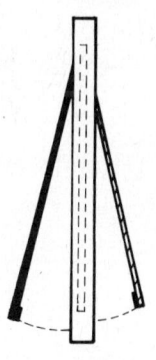

Grooming

A soft baby's hairbrush and steel comb should be bought, either from a pet-shop or a chemist. A regular brushing is adequate for short-haired breeds but the coats of long-hairs should be combed out daily to prevent tangles and fur balls.

Figure 25 Basic grooming equipment: *bristle brush, rubber brush and metal comb*

Toilet facilities

It is as well to have at hand a plastic cat-litter tray and a packet of cat-litter for house-training purposes. This is particularly important if the cat is to live in an upstairs flat as the tray will be in regular use.

Transporting your cat

If you intend to show your cat and/or to travel fairly extensively, baskets made of wire are well recommended. However, if your cat's journeys will be limited and you do not wish to invest in a carrying basket or holdall just for an occasional visit to the veterinary surgeon or cattery, animal rescue societies, such as the RSPCA, stock cardboard pet-carrying packs at reasonable cost.

Figure 26 Carrying basket

Means of identification

A metal disc engraved with your name and address and attached to your cat's collar should enable your cat to be returned to you should it stray. Do not confuse a cat collar with those marketed for toy dogs. A cat collar is elasticated so that it can expand in the event of its wearer getting caught on a branch or other obstacle; it is infinitely preferable to any other type.

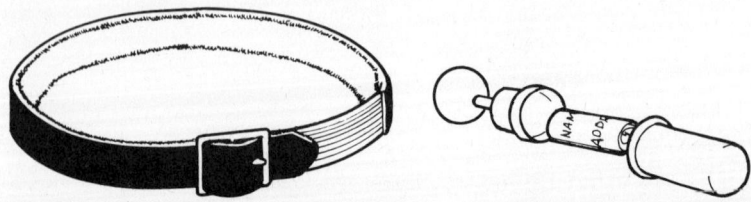

Figure 27 Velvet-lined collar with elastic inset for safety and identification capsule

For some years now, my Siamese has been wearing a capsule, which unscrews, attached to his collar. Inside, written on a piece of paper, are the words: 'My name is Samson, my owner loves me, generous reward if found' together with my name and address. I find it very reassuring to know that he is wearing this.

Other accessories

In both the UK and the USA, cat accessories have become very big business. After all, responsible owners want to buy all the things which a pet might need—not only a suitable basket, but blankets, feed bowls and toys—most of which will eventually need replacing.

In the UK, Harrods, the famous Knightsbridge department store, which boasts the ability to provide anything from an elephant to a grand piano, has a famous pet department which can generally supply an enviable range of feline place mats, bejewelled collars and novelty squeaky toys. Even so, it cannot, to my mind, compete with the pet department of Macy's, the equally famous store on Broadway, New York, which has the most varied supply of accessories imaginable. The American who wants his or her cat, or any other pet, to have everything, will almost certainly want to take a trip to Macy's, a visit being an outing in itself.

Although American manufacturers have some novel as well as practical items on offer and most pet-stores there can provide for the most discerning pet-owners' needs, the UK certainly does not lag behind.

A very popular service, for example, is provided by an enterprising young businessman called Anthony Green, a former journalist, who, not so many years ago, set up his own postal pet-shop, advertising extensively and inviting prospective customers to send for his catalogue *Pets Bazaar*. From his premises in Kilburn, north-west London, Mr Green now sends out thousands of catalogues every week and there is no doubt that his wares are universally popular with cat-owners.

On offer, for instance, are pussy holdalls, advertised as a smart and convenient way to carry your cat; a cat climbing-tree, which can be fitted in any room at a ceiling height of up to 2.75 m (9 ft), which it is said, will appeal to your cat's natural climbing instincts while affording the pleasure of watching its antics; a domestic cat harness, obviously aimed at the pure-bred and said to be more comfortable than a collar and lead; and a hopper-type food and water reservoir so that your cat will not go without during your absence.

Of course, if you are able to visit one or more of the large cat shows it is likely that accessory manufacturers will have taken space there and this is an excellent chance to see what is available.

3
Feeding

While many owners prefer to cater independently for their cats and kittens, it is important to point out that, in so doing, they are not necessarily providing an extra kindness. Proprietary brands of canned foods have been scientifically prepared to provide a balanced diet, as well as a convenient method of feeding, and all are supplemented with the necessary vitamins and minerals.

Adult cats

Cats, unlike dogs, are almost completely carnivorous and so they continue to have high protein and vitamin requirements even when fully grown. The adult diet, therefore, should still be based on animal foods with a small proportion of cereal. Many adult cats continue to enjoy milk, but many more are unable to digest it. Cat-owners often argue fiercely as to the merits and demerits of supplying milk rather than water as a drink. The answer is to provide water at all times and to give milk if the cat enjoys it. My own Siamese has phases of demanding a drink when he sees me pick up a milk bottle, whereas for weeks on end he will turn up his nose at such a drink if it is regularly provided.

It is particularly important never to give a cat milk or any other food straight from the refrigerator or cold larder. As a predator, the cat is used to a diet of warm food and will turn away from cold fare.

Just as one cat will revel in its daily saucer of milk and another will be content with a drink of water, so you will find that, while one adult cat thrives on one meal a day, another may require two or even three meals a day; this will do no harm as long as the cat is not allowed to overeat and become obese.

Since all cats are about the same size, the amount of food needed does not vary a great deal. Toms (entire or neutered) need about 300-350 calories a day, while the smaller queens require 200-250 calories. To work out or check your cat's diet, the following table gives a calorie equivalent of some common foods for cats.

Figure 28 Oriental Tabbies feeding: Lilac (left), Chocolate (right)

Common foods and their calorie equivalents

Type of food	Calories
Small tin, meat and jelly type	150
Small tin, fish and cereal type	200
Milk 114 cc (4 fl.oz.)	75
Cod, coley or rock salmon 225 g (8 oz)	250
Herring 225 g (8 oz)	350
Lean minced beef 225 g (8 oz)	375
Liver 57 g (2 oz)	75
Rabbit or chicken meat 225 g (8 oz)	300
Dried cat food 85 g (3 oz)	300

Apart from proprietary brands of tinned cat food, it is also possible to buy various types of soft moist convenience cat food, which will provide a full day's nourishment for an adult cat, or dry packeted cat food of the munchy variety, a cupful of which may be served either dry or moistened with milk or water; this again will provide the adult cat with a full day's nourishment. However, if you serve a dry food without moistening it first, it is essential to ensure that the cat has an ample supply of drinking water. Finally, although liver has long had a reputation as a cat's delicacy, do make sure that it is served only as a special treat and certainly no more than once a week because it acts as a purgative.

Just because your cat appears to relish one particular brand of cat food or painstakingly-prepared meal, do not make the mistake of serving the same food every day of the week. A cat, like a person, tires of a monotonous diet and, being a creature of habit, enjoys regular meals and varied menus.

Never serve sharp poultry bones or any bones which are likely to splinter and cause internal troubles. As far as farm cats are concerned, there is no truth in the idea that if they are unfed they will become good mousers. The best mousers are cats which are properly nourished.

Kittens

A kitten should normally remain with its mother until it is at least 6 weeks but preferably 8 weeks old, by which time the kittens should be weaned and able to eat a quarter to half of a 177 g (6¼ oz) tin of kitten food per day or, if you prefer, a similar quantity of cooked fish, minced raw meat or cooked rabbit, either plain or mixed with brown bread and barley. Pearl barley cooked with rabbit absorbs a lot of gravy and makes the dish particularly nourishing and tasty. Barley can be given on its own at one meal with rabbit gravy, or mixed with the rabbit. Another alternative might be cod's head and fresh haddock baked in the oven. The total quantity should be divided into four meals. The daily feeding chart shown overleaf should be helpful.

Many kittens enjoy a saucerful of milk, although a few individuals are unable to digest it properly. Clean drinking water should always be available whether or not milk is given and it is most important that any food left uneaten is thrown away. Keep the kitten's dishes apart from those of your family and wash them separately.

Daily food requirements for kittens

Age of kitten	Tins per day (177 g size)	Meals per day
Weaning to 8 weeks	¼ – ½	4
8 – 16 weeks	½ – ¾	3
16 – 20 weeks	¾ – 1	3
20 – 26 weeks	1 – 1½	2

Once your kitten is past 6 months of age it can be regarded as a cat and fed accordingly. However, while some adult cats are content with one meal a day, this is not advisable until your pet is at least 9 months old.

4
General care and training

If you talk about dog-training, those in the know will launch into a volume about obedience exercises and past experiences. If you speak of training a cat, they will merely give a wry smile for the cat or kitten lives with us by choice and will always retain its independence.

Nevertheless, it can be house-trained and this is a habit best achieved by placing it on a litter tray every time it has eaten or had a drink. However, there is little else it really needs to know and, with its keen intelligence, you may even find that it discovers the tray and realises its purpose before you have even reached lesson one.

Figure 29 Cream Burmese using litter tray

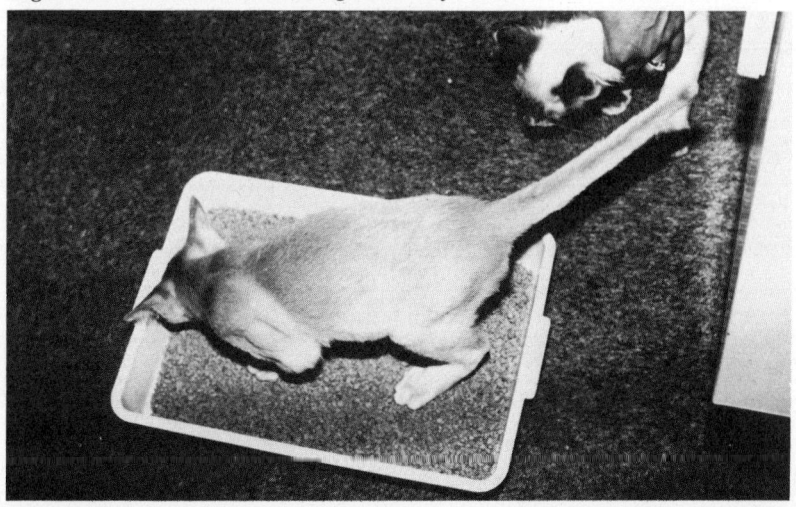

If a cat has made a mess on the floor, disinfect the area and eradicate the smell or your pet will foul the same area again and again. Unless you live in an upstairs apartment or adjacent to a busy street, you will want to let your kitten out into the garden after feeding and drinking, once it is bigger, stronger and less vulnerable. This will often be a natural transition, although there is the occasional dirty cat which requires a little more patience and perseverance than its fellows.

Kittens enjoy trying to catch their own reflection in a mirror and playing with a ping-pong ball, a soft toy or crumpled piece of paper. However, they will not think twice about sharpening their claws on the table leg or furniture covers if left unchecked. To prevent them from scratching the furniture, distract their attention from such articles and introduce them to a scratching post or similar item that has been provided for the purpose. Never punish a kitten or cat physically as it will never forget or forgive.

Figure 30 Kittens playing with toys

Do not allow the kitten to wander out of sight during the first few weeks and try gradually to establish a regular routine. If, for instance, it becomes accustomed to receiving a meal at 6 o'clock every evening you can be sure that it will appear a few minutes before this, maybe mewing and rubbing its body against your legs, just as the adult cat, if you establish a pattern of letting it in for the night at a certain time, as if by magic, will suddenly appear through the cat flap or be waiting on the window-sill or door-step. All too often the lost or stray cat is the result of an owner changing their routine with the result that the let-down cat wanders elsewhere in search of food and shelter.

Changes in routine brings me to the subject of holidays and other occasions which may take you away from home. At such times, arrangements must be made for the feeding and sheltering of your pet and, while it is possible to obtain food-hoppers which will supply a cat with food for up to 5 days, it must be accepted that even the best appliances fail and your cat could be left hungry until the day of your return.

Many owners whose cats are particularly attached to their homes, arrange for a neighbour to call while they are away and feed the cat at its regular time, which is all very well, provided warmth and other necessary facilities are always available. However, no matter how well-meaning the neighbours, circumstances can occur which preclude them from attending to the chore, again leaving a cat which is not only hungry but bewildered.

Without doubt, the best course is to book the cat into a cattery which has been recommended by your veterinary surgeon, an animal welfare society or a cat-loving friend whose own pet has a been a regular customer.

Standards of catteries vary but one would expect to find accommodation that has heating during the colder months, individual runs, a high standard of cleanliness, security, adequate ventilation and enough space for the cat to move around. Any cattery worth its salt will almost certainly insist on proof of inoculation against feline infectious enteritis (panleucopenia) and 'cat flu' which can be caused by several viruses. A demand for proof of inoculation should not be interpreted as fussiness. After all, you would be far from pleased if your cat were to pick up an infection from another resident.

It is essential when booking your own summer holiday, or if you expect to be away over a public holiday such as Christmas, to ring the cattery and book a place well in advance. It is usually possible to obtain a booking at reasonably short notice during the off-season, but at holiday periods the best catteries are always firmly booked months ahead.

A growing number of catteries are asking for an additional fee to cover the cost of insuring boarders against veterinary fees. Pet insurance generally is becoming more widely available. Veterinary attention can be expensive and sensible owners often feel that it is well worth making a modest annual outlay to an organisation specialising in this type of cover, such as the giant Pet Plan organisation in the UK. Breed clubs can sometimes offer this facility under a block policy for its members. Veterinary surgeons are usually most helpful in advising on suitable schemes.

Figure 31 Breeding quarters in a cattery

I have already touched on the importance of spaying queens and, unless you are definitely planning to use a tom for stud purposes, it also should be neutered at 4 to 6 months of age, although the operation can be carried out later.

An adult male cat tends to spray urine with a persistent unpleasant odour and to get injured in fights with other toms. Indeed, its psychological make-up is such that, un-neutered, it cannot suppress this warring instinct. Having it neutered prevents the heartbreak of seeing your pet coming home time and time again with torn ears and other nasty wounds.

5
The show world

What makes a show cat?

The majority of people who exhibit cats began from owning one pure-bred puss. They might have started by owning and exhibiting an attractive and well-cared for cross-breed because classes for pet cats are included in most shows. An owner may select a pure-bred cat for any number of reasons, ranging from admiration of a friend's Abyssinian or Burmese to seeing a picture of a certain variety and deciding no other will do.

Some people buy a pure-bred cat for the express purpose of showing it and, if it is a particularly good specimen, breeding from it. More often than not, however, owners get the show bug either after being persuaded to enter their cat in a show by a friend or the breeder, or by entering for the fun of the occasion and being surprised and encouraged by their success. Having made friends in the Fancy, they then move on to greater and more prestigious wins.

The Cat Fancy

In the UK, all pure-bred cats are judged by an official standard approved by the governing council of the Cat Fancy. All pure-bred cats which are exhibited must be registered with the Fancy. Owners receive a Certificate of Pedigree at the time of purchase and subsequently have ownership of the cat officially transferred from the breeder to themselves and recorded by the Fancy on payment of a small fee.

In the USA, the system is slightly more complicated. There is not a single governing body as in the UK but eight or more, each of which may have slight differences in its approved standard of points for the perfect cat. However, the general principle applies—that cats must be registered with a governing body before being entered in pure-bred classes. This means that, in the USA, it may be necessary to register a cat with several governing bodies if it is intended to exhibit it at shows run under the auspices of more than one body. Generally it is not the governing bodies themselves which organise cat shows, but, in a manner similar to that of the Kennel Club in the UK, they license a club to hold a show in return for a minimal fee.

Organisations in the United Kingdom

The birth of a governing body in the UK took place as early as 1871. This was when Mr Harrison Weir, aware of the following that cats had in the country, thought what a splendid idea it would be to organise a show where people might see the various types of beautiful cats available. It is on record that many thousands of people queued up in London's magnificent Crystal Palace, later to be tragically

Figure 32 National Cat Club Show, Olympia

destroyed by fire, to see the cats. Following this event, many people began to breed cats selectively, including Queen Victoria.

It was rare in those days to know the names of a cat's parents and grandparents, but it was soon discovered that, by mating cats of the same colour or coat patterns, kittens could be produced resembling the parents. Careful records were written out, giving details of each cat used for breeding and, before long, Certificates of Pedigree were being issued and it was possible to trace a cat's great-great-grandparents. As more Cat Shows were held, visitors came from all over the world to admire Britain's beautiful cats. Many bought prizewinners which they took to their homelands. The USA started to hold its own Cat Shows and soon cats were just as popular there. The popularity of the Fancy in the USA greatly increased after a successful show held in Madison Square Gardens, New York, in 1895. Today there are shows in many other parts of the world, but the largest is still in the UK where over 2000 cats appear annually at the National Cat Club Show at Olympia, London.

The National Cat Club was established in 1887, with the aim of promoting and breeding pure-bred cats and running Cat Shows. In 1898, Lady Marcus Beresford formed a rival organisation, the Cat Club, the aims of which were identical. For 7 years, the Cat Club bravely struggled on. It did not measure up to the task and the National Cat Club again reigned supreme, but there was more competition to come in the form of another newly-formed group, the Cat Fanciers Association. In 1910, following much squabbling between cat-lovers, a conference of interested parties was called at which agreement to form the Governing Council of the Cat Fancy was reached. The general meeting of this august body was held at the Inns of Court Hotel, London, on 11 October, 1910. Seventy years later, it is still the powerful Governing Council of the Cat Fancy which provides for the registration of cats and cat pedigrees, classifies cat breeds, approves cat shows and does all within its power to improve cat-breeding and welfare in the UK.

The Council has a large number of affiliated Cat Clubs all of which may, when their membership totals 100 persons, appoint a delegate to the Council. They may appoint two delegates if membership reaches 150 but, should it fall below the required figures, the Club loses its right to representation. However, some historic specialist clubs, such as the Siamese Cat Club, are allowed representation irrespective of membership level.

Organisations in the United States of America

Although there are quite a number of governing bodies in the USA and, indeed, a separate body in Canada (the Canadian Cat Association or CCA), the main organisations are probably the Cat Fanciers Federation Inc. (CFF) in Schenectady, New York and the Cat Fanciers Association (CFA) in New Jersey.

The Cat Fanciers Federation Inc., since 1919, has provided registration services, devised rules by which shows are run and adopted standards of perfection, always bearing in mind that the welfare and betterment of the cat are its ultimate goals. The founders established an organisation based on the principle of equal representation. This concept at the time was a radical change and is still one feature in which the CFF differs strikingly from other organisations.

An executive board composed of one delegate or proxy per Club forms the governing body of the Federation. Member clubs are encouraged to take an active part by submitting their ideas in the form of proposals. These in turn are circulated to all other Clubs where they are studied and voting instructions given to their representatives. In this way all decisions are made by a majority vote of the entire membership. CFF is proud of its clear concise show rules. These result in smoothly-run shows which are enjoyable to the exhibitor.

The number of shows sponsored by the CFF Clubs increases each year and testifies to member involvement and enthusiasm. All shows are scored for the parade of perfection and the Federation urges its member clubs to provide all-American scoring as a benefit to exhibitors.

The Federation maintains a panel of top judges who are tested yearly for their awareness of changes in the Show rules and standards. Supplementing an already good team, there are competent judges from other associations with whom the Federation has reciprocal agreements. As an added bonus, the Federation's rigid judges' training programme brings forth able new judges from time to time. Indeed the CFF has sought to refrain from extremes in all areas, without closing their eyes to new ideas that come along. Updating is a never-ending process, whether it is registration rules, acceptance of new breeds and/or colours, improvements of the judging standards, or amendments to the by-laws, their boast being that any of their members or their officers will be pleased to tell you why *they* choose the CFF and find it to their liking; new members, of course, are encouraged.

The Cat Fanciers Association of New Jersey was organised in 1906 with the following objectives: improvement of the breed of cat, the registration of pedigrees of cats and kittens, the promulgation of rules for the management of cat shows, the licencing of cat shows held under the rules of the organisation and the promotion of the interests of breeders and exhibitors of all cats. Later a most important objective was added, the promotion of the welfare of all cats.

The CFA held its first shows during 1906, one in Buffalo and one in Detroit. In 1909, the CFA published the first stud book and register in the *Cat Journal*. Also in 1909, Volume I of the Stud Book was published in book form. CFA held its first annual meeting in 1907 at Madison Square Gardens, New York. The fundamental principle of CFA at this time was home rule and this policy has held throughout the years. On 13 December 1913, the Empire Cat Club—the CFA's oldest club—was organised and has remained a faithful member of the Association through the years. On 18 September 1919, articles of incorporation were drawn up under the laws of the State of New York. The CFA then entered a new and successful era and the Association has grown steadily.

The CFA has no individual membership: breeders and exhibitors remain members of local clubs that are affiliated with the Association. In 1962, a total of 129 clubs was affiliated with CFA. In October 1978, club memberships totalled 604 in the USA, Canada and Japan. The affairs of the Association are managed by the Executive Board, which consists of the President, Executive Vice-President, Secretary, Treasurer, 7 Regional Directors and 7 Directors-at-large. The officers and Directors-at-large are elected by delegates to the annual meeting held in June of each year; the 7 Regional Directors are elected by mail ballot by the member Clubs in each of the CFA's 7 regions. This 18-member Executive Board represents all areas of the country.

The CFA has given awards to the top cats, top kittens and top premiership cats for many years. The Hydon-Goodwin Challenge Awards, which honour each top-scoring cat in several categories with a $25.00 government bond, have grown to become CFA National awards with $500.00 as a monetary award for the best cat, together with a plaque. Monetary awards and plaques are presented to the top twenty cats, the top five kittens and top five cats in premiership at the Annual Awards Banquet held in conjunction with the Annual Meeting in June. This affair has become a highlight of the Annual Meeting with over 400 fanciers attending the presentation and the colour-slide show of the winning cats. CFA has grown in all areas and approximately 260 shows were held last season in all areas of North America, Hawaii and Japan. The CFA Shows are judged by individuals who have completed a rigorous training programme that well qualifies them to evaluate the show cat.

Figure 33 Self Red British Long-hair with rosette

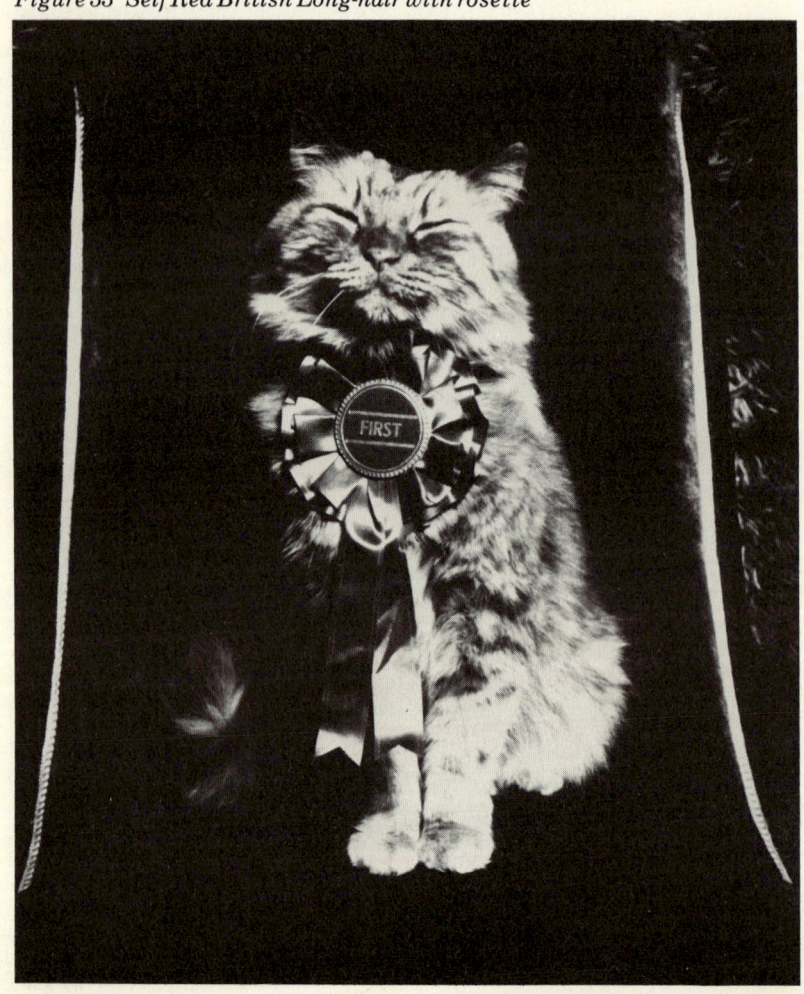

Types of classes and awards

Basically all cats are judged by a standard of perfection, 100 marks being those attributable to a perfect example of the type or variety; such marks are given for the exhibit with the right shape of head, ears, body and fur according to the standard laid down by the official body.

A cat that wins three certificates, under three different judges, can become a Champion. A cat may become a Grand Champion by winning three Champion Challenge Certificates, at three shows, under three different judges, but before entering a Grand Champion Class, the exhibit must be a full Champion. Neutered cats can be exhibited in Neuter Classes and become what is known as a Premier by winning at three shows under different judges and a Grand Premier under the same rules and conditions as those laid down for a Grand Champion. Judges carefully examine the condition of each entry, assessing the head, shape and colour of eyes, ears, body, tail and also the colour pattern of the fur where this applies.

In the UK, all pedigree varieties for which an official standard has been approved also have an allotted breed number (see p. 00). Breeders enjoy trying to develop cats with new colours and of different coat and type, a habit which, in the past, has led to very large entries at cat shows of exhibits for which no actual standard existed. In such cases, cats are registered as: Long-hairs—13a Any Other Colour; Short-hairs—26 Any Other Variety; Any Other Colour Siamese—32x. The practice now, however, is for such new varieties to be placed on an experimental register and given a provisional standard. Provisional recognition and a breed name may follow as numbers and quality increase, but Championship status is only granted when one hundred breed members have been bred to standard. Meanwhile such exhibits are entered in what are known as Assessment Classes. These cats are not judged against other exhibits but on individual merit and the number of Merit Certificates awarded help towards the official recognition of the breed.

In a large Championship Show, there may also be classes run by individual cat clubs (such as the Chocolate-pointed Siamese Cat Club, who might have classes for the best Chocolate-pointed Siamese cat, kitten and neuter) as well as classes for the various types and colours of British short-haired cats, short-haired neuters and so on. Often there is a non-pedigree section for unregistered cats, kittens and neuters which afford the proud owner of a well-loved cross-breed, and often a child with a well-cared-for pet, an opportunity to win an award for the general appearance, appeal and condition of their pet; such sections often include such worthwhile classes as 'Any Variety of Rescued Cat or Kitten', 'The Cat or Kitten with the Most Expressive Eyes', 'The Friendliest Cat or Kitten' and so on, thus ensuring that the Cat Show has something to offer not only the breeder-exhibitor, but also the little boy or girl whose pet is the apple of their eye.

Figure 34 Blue Long-hair being bathed prior to a show

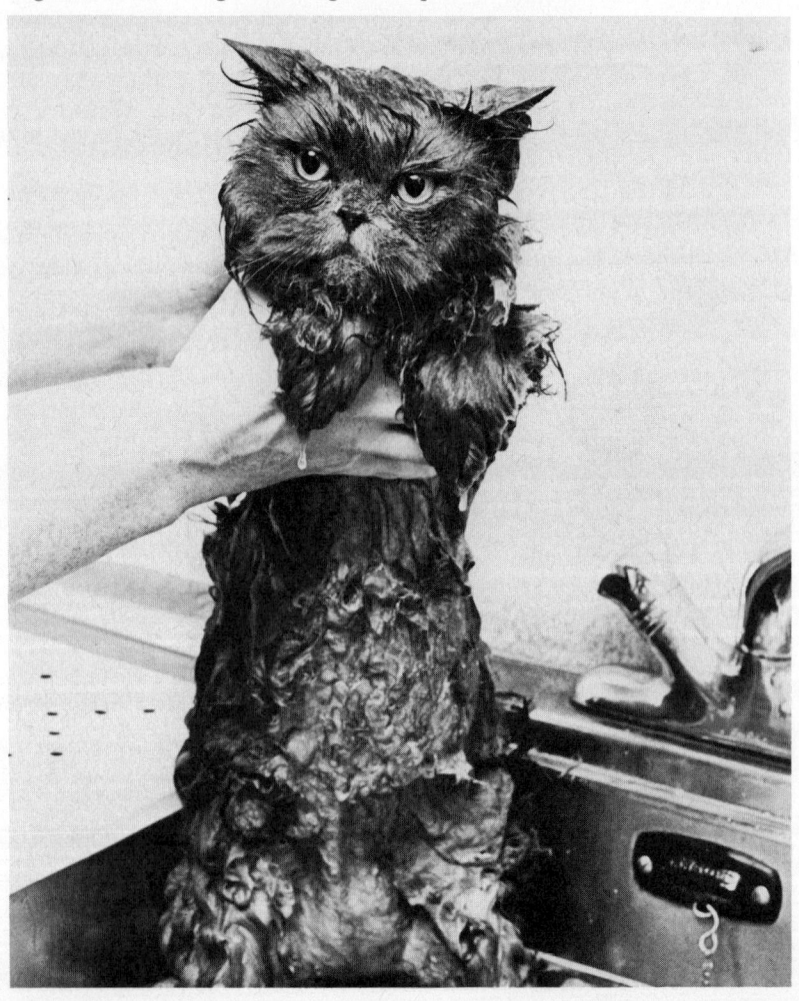

Showing systems in the UK and USA vary considerably, both in methods of judging and composition of classes, a fact which makes it all the more important for potential exhibitors to visit a show run under the auspices of the governing body before going ahead and making an entry.

Figure 35 Combing out a Blue Long-hair before a show

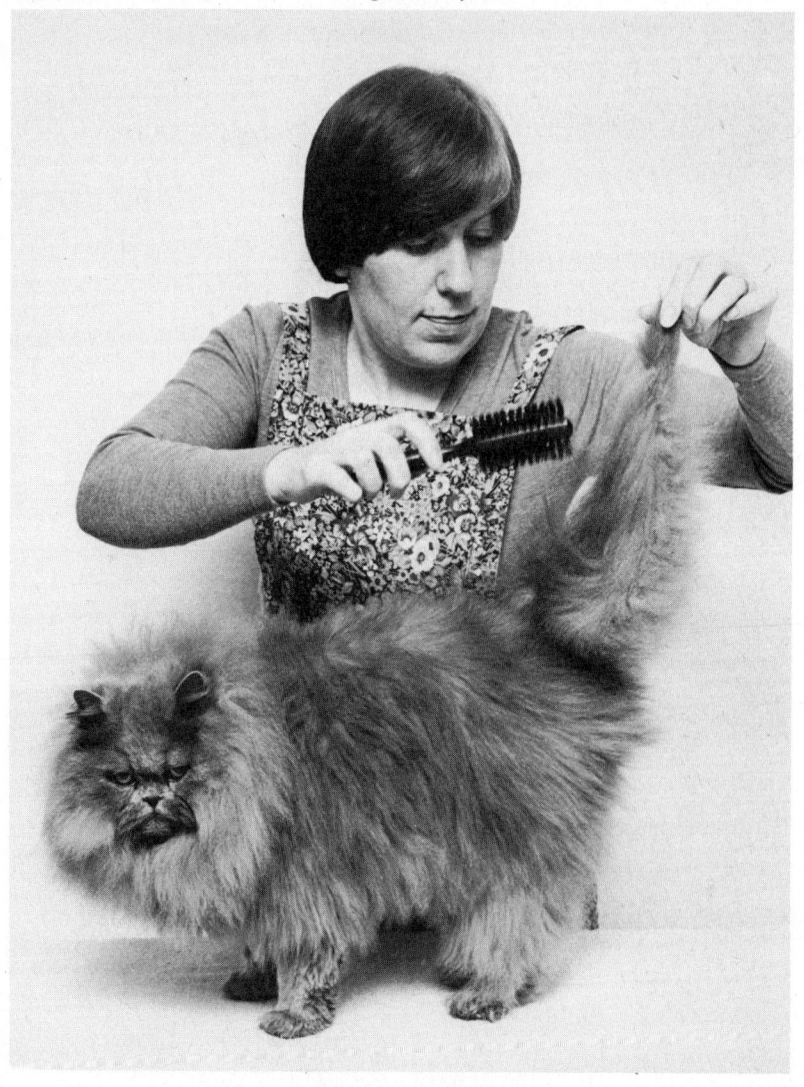

In the UK, for example, the cats are judged in their pens while their owners remain outside the hall and the steward pushes the judge's table from exhibit to exhibit as the cats are examined by the judge. The cats must all be shown on a plain white blanket with no distinguishing marks or bright accessories. The results are subsequently pinned up on a board and prize cards and rosettes are pinned to the pens at a later stage.

In the USA, judging takes place in a ring with the cats in numbered pens and, as the judges do not visit the exhibits in their ordinary pens during judging, these may be decorated as lavishly as their owners wish. Winners' ribbons are awarded immediately after judging. There are also marked differences in the manner in which Championship and Premiership status is obtained.

In the USA, before a cat may become a Champion or Premier, it has to win an Open Class for its breed and colour at least four or six times (according to the rules of the Association) under different judges. However, because shows are run on different lines, it is easier for a cat to achieve this status than it is in the UK, so the awards do not carry the same prestige. Much more valuable are the titles of Grand Champion or Premier, for which a cat must accumulate a number of points at a series of shows awarded on the basis of the number of other champions it has beaten.

Figure 36 Award-winning cat in a show pen

Could you become a judge?

Obviously it is necessary for a judge to have seen many hundreds of cats of a specific variety over the years to be able to tell, from a swift appraisal and examination, which exhibits most nearly fulfil the standard of perfection laid down for their breed. You are unlikely to be able to do this unless you have also had experience as a breeder or exhibitor.

What exactly constitutes a potential judge varies, of course, according to the governing body, but usually a judge should have had a minimum of 3 or 5 years experience in the variety and, in some cases, may be required to have a number of champions to his or her credit.

Figure 37 Judge and steward examining a Cream Long-hair at the judging table

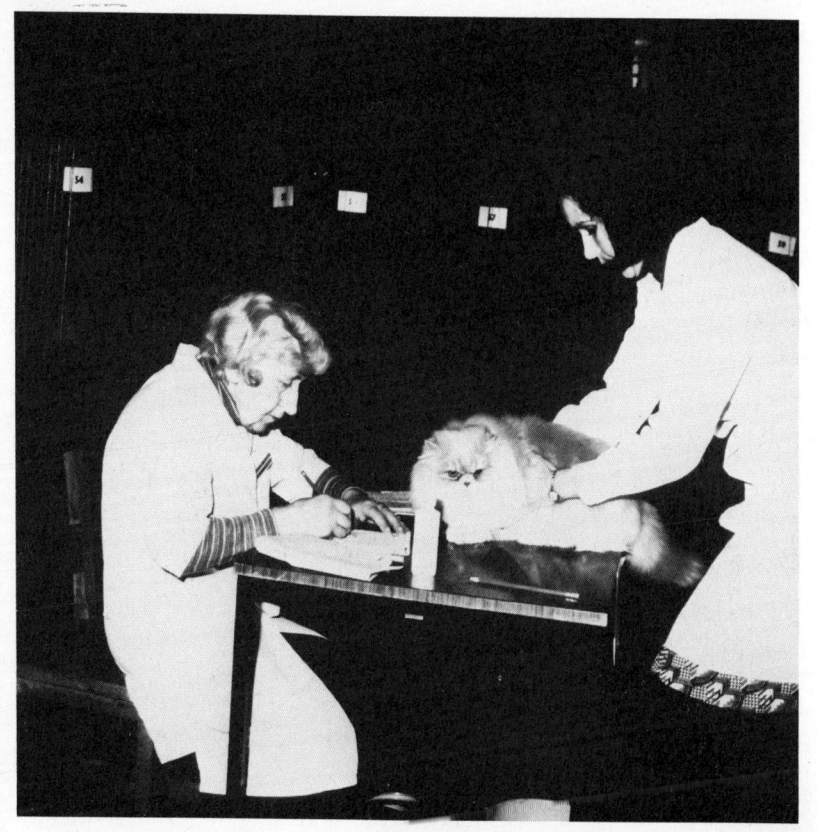

Some Associations demand experience as a judge's steward or clerk, as well as personal assessments of the candidate's knowledge and skill. Others require written and practical examinations to be taken. In some cases, the next stage is to act as a probationer judge, who is permitted to judge only kittens for 2 years before becoming fully qualified to judge one or two breeds. In the UK, a judge receives no payment other than hotel and travelling expenses but many clubs elsewhere pay a fee per show or per cat judged.

It would seem that, apart from an enthusiasm for the Fancy and involvement as an exhibitor or breeder, stewarding is the best introduction and stepping-stone to the judging role. In the UK, the steward, apart from ensuring that the necessary equipment is on the judge's trolley or table, must see that the judge's book is written up before his/her arrival, with the number of classes and exhibits to be judged, and, when the judging of each class is completed, that the judge has signed the tear-off slips signifying the winners. The steward then takes these to the secretary's table.

Being constantly at the judge's side, the steward, regardless of country or governing body, is able to observe at first-hand the appraisal given to each cat and the allocation of marks, until he finds himself automatically, and independently, arriving at similar decisions.

6
Breeding

First of all, I would like to dispel the theory once and for all that there is one method of breeding a pet animal and another of a creature for show. There is only one way to breed and that is the correct way.

Domestic pets, including the cat, have a standard of excellence laid down by their Fancy's governing body or bodies, by which show exhibits are judged. It is hoped that animals will be bred to meet this standard and those people who are conscientious in their aim to produce pure-bred cats, or any other domestic animal which has a standard, should mate only males and females which conform as closely as possible to the standard. This does not mean that the resultant litter will consist solely of show prospects but it should include one or more animals which are; the others perhaps will fall short in some minor detail, such as colour or length of tail, and may be offered to loving homes as pure-bred pets.

In my opinion, and probably that of most others who view the subject responsibly, to breed cats, dogs, or any other domestic animal from inferior stock is totally undesirable, for not only are the offspring unlikely to be any better than their ancestors, but such indiscriminate breeding could start a continuing faulty line and the perpetuation of hereditary faults. Also, considering that cats multiply thirty to forty-five times more rapidly than human beings and that one female cat, in 5 years, can give rise to some 20 000 descendants, many of which can only expect a life of misery, hunger, disease and terror, the desirability of neutering every cat not wanted for breeding purposes becomes quite obvious.

Should you decide to let your female cat have a litter, then the following information should be of help.

The young queen will first come into season when she is just over 6 months old. Her restlessness, persistent mewing and rolling about will be probably your only indication that she is in season. If she is mated successfully, her kittens will be born 9 weeks later.

Mating

Mating a pure-bred cat is, of course, somewhat different from the unscheduled liaison between a tabby queen and the ginger tom next door. The owner of, say, a Siamese queen, will locate a suitable stud tom through the pages of a club magazine or by visiting a cat show. After paying the required stud fee, the owner takes the queen to the stud (the tom always performs best on his own territory), where she will remain until her pregnancy is reasonably certain.

Some pure-bred cats can command quite a sizeable sum. However, it is unlikely that a solitary female would produce more than a little pocket money for her owner, considering the cost of petrol, the distance involved in getting to the stud and the stud fee and veterinary costs that may be incurred. The concensus of opinion is that, to make any money out of cats, one really needs to run a fully-fledged cattery, keeping a number of females and a stud cat, and perhaps running a boarding cattery as a side-line.

Pregnancy

The pregnant cat needs special attention as regards food, which should be clean, wholesome and given as many small meals rather than one or two large ones. A daily teaspoonful of cod-liver oil in food and a yeast tablet (such as 'Kitzyme') will be beneficial. Lumpy food should not be given. The queen will need more to drink than usual, much handling should be avoided and she should never be lifted up carelessly.

While the cat will need only slightly increased rations during the early stages of pregnancy these should be stepped up when she is near to kittening. By the time she is feeding her kittens, she should be consuming as much as two or three times her normal rations. Again, I would stress that one of the branded, complete cat foods on the market will provide all the vitamins necessary for your pet and her family, but at this time you must also provide her with a generous supply of milk to drink. Do not give table scraps, even if this is your custom, for she will benefit far more from protein, vitamins and minerals. Liver and/or a cooked egg included with meals will increase her protein intake.

Once the kittens are weaned the diet should gradually be reduced until the queen is again having her normal once or twice daily meals.

Kittening

Shortly before giving birth the queen will begin to look for a comfortable and likely nursery. A large, lidless wooden box turned on its side with a narrow board fastened across the front, near the floor, to prevent the kittens falling out, is suitable. This should be placed in a quiet corner out of draughts. The bedding should be soft and clean. Newspaper should not be used unless well covered, e.g. by soft white paper or flannel. Printing ink is poisonous and the mother cat can ingest it by licking the kittens whose coats have been in direct contact with it.

Figure 38 A kittening box made out of an old tea chest

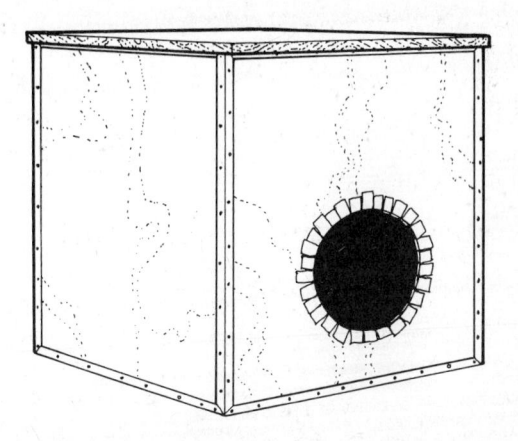

Do not be surprised, however, if your queen has quite different ideas about where she wishes to give birth. If you are not careful, this may be in the foot of your linen cupboard, in a space under your kitchen sink or even in a garden shed. If, therefore, the queen goes missing at about the time when her litter is due, do search diligently for her but remember that she must be kept absolutely quiet and undisturbed. It is quite common for the mother cat to lift her kittens up gently by the scruff of the neck and remove them from the place which you have chosen to another which she prefers.

Generally, there are three to six kittens in a litter and they are born within a few hours of the beginning of labour. The queen will do all that is necessary to wash the kittens and clean them afterwards. However, if she appears to be straining for an undue length of time without producing a kitten, do seek immediate veterinary advice. When the kittens have been born and licked clean, give the mother a warm milky drink and then leave her in peace as much as possible for the next 2 weeks. By then the kittens' eyes will be open, but they will be sensitive to strong light.

Weaning

The kittens will be feeding from their mother until they are 4 weeks old. Warm milk, either on its own or mixed with a baby cereal such as 'Farex', can provide a useful weaning food. The greater proportion of the diet, however, should consist of meat or fish in some form. Provide both to prevent your kittens from becoming addicted to one food. This is a particular danger with liver, which cats find highly palatable. Tinned kitten foods, introduced gradually, will provide a balanced diet.

Figure 39 Lilac Point Siamese with kittens

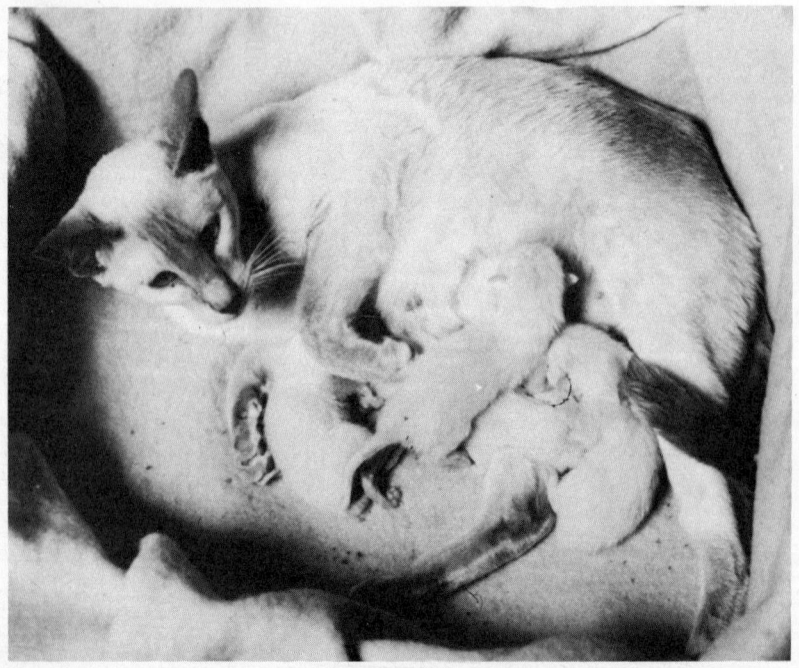

Watching kittens at weaning is a delightful if messy spectacle until the young ones have developed the knack of licking from a dish. It is best to start them off by dipping a finger into some milky substance and putting it repeatedly to the kitten's mouth. Do not make the mistake of dipping a kitten's mouth into the milk thinking that it will start lapping. The kitten could sniff the milk up its nose and become frightened.

Take the kittens away from the mother once a day while you are feeding them individually. After a few days, provide two milk meals daily gradually increasing to three and finally four meals, introducing solid food. Make absolutely sure that they are well able to handle solid food before they go to their new homes.

7
You, your cat and the law

The position of the cat in law is somewhat complex and, indeed, can vary, not only from country to country, but, in the USA, from state to state. There are, for instance, some cities in the USA where owners are required to keep cats indoors and exercise them only on a lead. In the UK, however, owners cannot even be held legally responsible for damage done by their cat, for instance, where a neighbour has complained of a cat entering a garden and digging up seeds, as it is understood that the cat has a 'free spirit' and the owner cannot reasonably be expected to restrain it. A motorist in the UK, who has the misfortune to run over a dog is legally bound to report the incident to the police. If he has run over a cat, however, he has no legal obligation to do anything, although one would hope he might feel morally bound to move the body to the side of the road or call a veterinary surgeon if the animal is injured.

The Animals' Act of 1971 does render an owner liable if a cat with a record of viciousness attacks a third party; if it is an isolated incident, no liability is held as it is considered that the owner could not be expected to know that the animal would behave in such a manner. There are strict anti-cruelty laws in the UK, which in certain American states apply only to deliberate or unnecessary cruelty. Whereas it is considered illegal to abandon an animal in the UK, this is not the case in some American states.

Despite what may sometimes appear as the complete disregard for cats in law, you can, nonetheless, in most places and circumstances, be taken to task for harbouring so many cats as to cause nuisance or smell. Where quarantine regulations exist, it is, of course, forbidden to bring a cat into the country without making arrangements for it to spend the allotted quarantine period in a Government-approved quarantine boarding establishment.

Animal law is indeed complex and, if one is likely to be involved in litigation, it is as well to enquire of a welfare society for the name of a legal adviser accustomed to handling briefs of this type.

Because it is not always possible to obtain as much assistance in finding a lost cat as one would wish—for instance, in the UK, police will help to find a lost dog but not a cat—some owners, as well as resorting to collar and disc (see p. 00), are also taking advantage of schemes whereby their cat has an identifying tattoo placed in a strategic position, so that, if it should turn up in a welfare shelter or laboratory, the code or, in the UK, the owner's National Insurance number, marked on the cat, can be linked quickly and efficiently with the name and address of its owner. In the UK, this scheme was initially introduced by a Miss Valerie Pratt under the auspices of the Central Dog Registry, but before long owners of cats and other animals were taking advantage of the service. A scheme on somewhat similar lines is provided by the I.D. Pet Service Center in Connecticut and addresses of both organisations are to be found at the back of this book.

8
Health and commonsense care

Cats are generally very healthy animals and many live long happy lives rarely needing veterinary attention. One is always reluctant to advise the owner of a cat just how long a pet is likely to live. Cats generally live for an average of 12 years, but a cat of 15 or even 20 years is not a rarity. The Siamese is particularly well-known for its longevity, but the cross-bred moggie obtained as a kitten from a nearby farm could live just as long.

The cat seems to have great self-curative and recuperative powers, often hiding away until some wound caused in a fight begins to heal, eating grass to help itself vomit, or remaining of its own accord indoors and sleeping in the warm until its normal good health is restored.

Nevertheless, if a cat shows symptoms of illness you should not wait 2 or 3 days to see if it recovers, but take it to a veterinary surgeon right away. It is far better to go to some small expense and, in your own estimation, possibly waste the veterinary surgeon's time, than to wait until a potentially serious condition is too far advanced to cure.

Nowadays, most veterinary surgeons appreciate clients taking their pets to the surgery rather than requesting a home call. However, few practitioners object to making a visit in the case of an emergency.

It is best to ring the surgery first as the receptionist will be able to tell you the surgery hours and perhaps give you a specific time to attend, because many veterinary surgeons are now working on a strict appointment basis. Obviously, however, in the case of an emergency, such as a road accident, injured animals will receive immediate attention.

As a spare-time official of an animal welfare society for many years, I receive hundreds of letters each week requesting advice on general pet care. Reading them, nearly always from well-meaning people, I never cease to be amazed by the many owners who, while professing to care for their pets, try out every conceivable remedy obtainable at the pet-shop, after making their own diagnosis, rather than go to what they consider the unnecessary expense of seeking veterinary advice and treatment. This is the height of idiocy when often they are spending many more times the cost of a veterinary surgeon's fee buying products designed to ease or cure a quite different malady and are often doing very much more harm than good.

Unfortunately, there is no National Health Service for cats but it is possible to take out an insurance to cover veterinary fees (see p. 00). However, a number of organisations, such as the People's Dispensary for Sick Animals, give free veterinary treatment in hardship cases or merely ask for a donation.

However, in grumbling, often unjustifiably, about veterinary fees, few people seem to realise that these must vary according to the overheads of the individual practice. This means that you are likely to pay more for veterinary treatment in the equivalent of Harley Street, London, or in New York's East Side, than you are in a less expensive neighbourhood.

The first rule must be to establish a friendly relationship with a veterinary surgeon from the time you first acquire your kitten. Always keep his address and telephone number handy and never dose the cat yourself while trusting to luck that you are doing the right thing.

Major diseases

Inoculations

When you have acquired your kitten, it would be sensible to consult your veterinary surgeon about inoculation against 'cat flu'. Probably he will suggest an initial inoculation at 6 weeks to 8 weeks of age and another when the kitten reaches 12 weeks; thereafter, booster jabs are recommended at 2-yearly intervals and, indeed, reputable catteries will not accept a cat boarder without proof of up-to-date inoculation. Please, however, do not regard the time intervals I have stated as being gospel, for there is often some variance in the recommended periods adopted from country to country and even from surgery to surgery.

There is a high mortality rate in kittens from each of several 'cat flu' viruses and, as these are extremely infectious, it is only fair on your pet to give him or her the best possible protection.

Cat distemper

This is similar in many ways to dog distemper but it is not the same disease. Cats and dogs cannot infect one another with distemper. Symptoms consist of running eyes and nose, with sneezing, and later the digestion and lungs may be affected. The cat should be kept quiet and warm and veterinary help sought at once. Although not so deadly as enteritis, many cats die of distemper and they can be saved only by immediate treatment and careful nursing. Loss of appetite makes feeding difficult and glucose injections may be necessary to maintain strength. The addition of strong-smelling substances, such as fish paste, to the invalid diet may encourage the sick cat to take food.

As in the case of human influenza, there are some years when the disease is not much worse than a bad cold while in other years it becomes dangerously virulent. Cats of all ages are able to catch it and it is more likely to occur in catteries or pet-shops, where cats live in crowded conditions.

Infectious feline enteritis, panleukopenia or cat fever

This is the most serious of all cat diseases which, when it appears in a neighbourhood, spreads so quickly, causing so many cats to die within a few days, that people often imagine that there has been malicious poisoning. Young cats, Persians and Siamese, are particularly susceptible and the disease is commonest in summer. The illness comes on suddenly with a rise of temperature to 40°C (103°F). The cat refuses food, sits huddled up, often near a water bowl or sink, but without taking water. It vomits occasionally, cries faintly when picked up and passes blood-stained motions. Death is likely to occur within 48 hours, often much sooner. Any cats which survive are immune for life. A vaccine is available which gives protection.

Pneumonitis

This is a severe disease of the upper respiratory tract. The symptoms are much like those for viral rhinotracheitis (see over) and consist of fever, sneezing, running eyes and nose; however, they last longer. Only your veterinary surgeon can distinguish and prescribe medication. Antibiotics are usually effective if you seek help soon enough.

Viral rhinotracheitis

This disease gives rise to much the same symptoms as a common cold in human beings. It is usually mild in adult cats, but can be serious in kittens. Keep your cat quiet indoors and out of draughts for a few days. If there is no marked improvement consult your veterinary surgeon.

Common problems and complaints

Abscesses

Daily brushing will show up any abscesses, swelling or wound which may be hidden in long fur and for which veterinary treatment might be needed.

Figure 40 Cat wearing an Elizabethan collar to prevent it scratching an infected ear

Accidents

If a cat suffers a scald or a burn as a result of a mishap in the kitchen, immediately hold the injured part under a slow-running cold tap for about 1 minute. This will be very helpful in reducing pain, shock and subsequent scarring. Afterwards, obtain professional help quickly.

In the case of road accidents, the animal should be kept in as natural a position as possible in case any bones are broken or there are internal injuries. It should be supported with one hand under the brisket, while the other holds the scruff of the neck; the legs should hang free. Gently place the cat in a suitable container for transport to the surgery.

Anal glands
Very often the cat which habitually rubs its backside along the ground is thought to be suffering from worm infestation (p. 00). Sometimes, however, the cat is attempting to alleviate irritation from the anal glands, two small sacs on either side of the anus. Such irritation is quite a common occurrence because, in both dogs and cats, the glands can become infected with yellow, foul-smelling liquid which is secreted in the sacs. Experienced owners may learn the knack of emptying these sacs themselves with nothing more than their fingers and a piece of cotton wool or tissue. Ask your veterinary surgeon to perform the task initially and, if you lack the nerve to do it yourself thereafter, you will only be joining the ranks of many other clients who regularly have this task undertaken for their pets.

Bathing
There is no need to bath a cat unless it is absolutely filthy. Indeed, it may panic if you do so. However, if a bath is an absolute necessity, make sure that the water temperature does not exceed 26°C (80°F), and rub a little petroleum jelly round the cat's eyes to prevent water from getting into them. Frankly, you would be better to use one of several good brands of dry shampoo which are on the market and available from nearly every chemist.

Constipation
This may be caused by hairballs (accumulation of hair that the cat licks from its coat) or improper diet. Older cats are more prone to this complaint than young ones. A teaspoonful of salad oil or butter and a meal of raw liver are very likely to do the trick, but if the cat squats and strains very often with no result, the trouble is likely to be urinary calculi (bladder or kidney stones) instead of constipation. In that case do not give a laxative. Take the patient to the veterinary surgeon immediately. It is serious.

Digestive complaints and hairball
In slight cases of these troubles, the cat will provide its own remedy by eating grass and town cats should be provided with a patch of grass growing in a window-box or in the yard. Constipation may be relieved by a tablespoonful of medicinal paraffin. This dose can be repeated, twice daily for 2 days. For any more serious digestive upset, veterinary advice should be sought at once.

Diarrhoea
This can be a minor upset or a symptom of something more serious. If it persists longer than 36 hours consult your veterinary surgeon. Do not give milk or raw liver as either may aggravate the condition.

Parasites
Fleas and lice can be controlled by commercial powders or sprays, but be sure to select a preparation made especially for cats. Some insecticides are fatal if swallowed and cats constantly lick their coats. Never use on or near a cat, anything containing creosote, naphthalene, tar, phenol, carbolic acid, creolin, DDT or chlordane. Even a minute quantity of DDT, carbolic acid or any tar derivative can kill a cat. To be safe, check with your veterinary surgeon. Flea collars have proved successful but some animals are extremely sensitive to the insecticides in them, so if you do use such a collar, inspect under it frequently for signs of irritation. Also watch for symptoms of illness or bizarre behaviour. Any collar is dangerous to a cat unless it will break apart or stretch to permit the cat to escape if it gets caught when the animal is climbing (see p. 42).

Ticks can be a serious problem, best left to your veterinary surgeon. Ear mites need veterinary attention also; the ears are delicate and mites can be painful. Internal parasites which may manifest themselves as small skin eruptions must also be watched for, especially if your cat is in contact with other animals or if you adopt a stray. Your veterinary surgeon can advise and check a faeces sample if necessary.

Putting to sleep
Well-cared for cats can live happily to a great age, sometimes for more than 20 years. If there is any painful disability, incurable illness or severe injury, however, they should be gently put to sleep. This can easily be done by the veterinary surgeon or the RSPCA or ASPCA clinic. No untrained person should put a cat to sleep and, in most places, it is an offence to attempt to kill any animal by improper means.

Teeth
Older cats should have their teeth checked for signs of tartar. This can cause considerable discomfort to the animal and affect its general health. If you find your pet's breath generally offensive, it is possible to obtain products, such as animal 'Amplex', which will help to relieve the condition.

Vomiting

Unless this is accompanied by other signs of illness, it is not necessarily serious. Cats vomit easily, for example to expel a hairball or some undigested grass. If vomiting persists, or if the cat shows other symptoms, such as loss of appetite, sluggishness, coughing, sneezing or gagging, take it to your veterinary surgeon immediately.

Worms

I once received a letter from a well-intentioned owner saying that her keen hunter cat appeared to be suffering from worms and that she had given the poor creature twenty-six different varieties of tablets over a frighteningly short period, believing she was doing the right thing. Ask your veterinary surgeon to prescribe pills for this complaint. These can be administered easily in the cat's food and will not prove expensive. I generally find that the best method of administering pills is by breaking and crushing them in the middle of a favourite delicacy. However, if your cat is like a bloodhound at detecting the most well-concealed medicament and persistently spits it out, you can try holding its head firmly with one hand, slightly tilted back; holding the pill in the other hand, you open the jaw and place it as far back on the tongue as possible.

9
Animal cemeteries

By some cruel twist of fate, the lifespan of a cat is not like that of Man, three score years and ten, but instead between 12 and 20 years. So we must, alas, steel ourselves for the sad day when our cat will no longer be found waiting at the door to be let in, or sitting on its favourite cushion by the fireside.

Every pet-owner cherishes the hope that, when the time comes, their pet will pass peacefully away in its sleep. Alas, this rarely happens and one must, eventually, make the selfless decision that it would be kinder for a cat to be put painlessly to sleep by a veterinary surgeon, if possible with its owner beside it so that it may be caressed as it falls peacefully into its final sleep.

This brings me to the equally painful subject of disposal. The veterinary surgeon, whether your pet is put to sleep in your own home or at his surgery will, as a matter of course, agree to dispose of the pet's body in accordance with whatever arrangements exist with the authorities in the area. You can rest assured also that, whatever these may be, every dignity is observed.

There are pet-owners, however, who want the companion who has shared their life for so long to be buried and here problems may arise if their home does not have a garden. There is, incidentally, no legal objection to anyone burying a pet in their own garden but the law does prohibit pets from being buried in sanctified ground alongside the remains of their owners.

There have for some time been pet memorial parks and cemeteries in the USA, a number of which are run by the Bide-A-Wee Home Association, which has offices in New York City and Long Island. It

Figure 41 A fitting end for a faithful companion

was in recognition of the deep emotion of many pet-owners at the death of an animal, that Bide-A-Wee established its Memorial Parks many years ago. Since then, many thousands of saddened pet-owners have found a tangible means of expressing their loss and immortalising their love, through interment of their pets in the Parks. The fees for the service aid the living through Bide-A-Wee's adoption programme for misplaced pets.

There are, in fact, more than 400 pet cemeteries in the USA and, to quote Maxwell Riddle, a renowned writer on dogs: 'Some of these are marginal operations, many are not'.

The first animal burial ground in the USA was established in 1896 in Hartsdale, New York, where the cost of interment starts at about £100 ($200). Here, among the pets of other notable people, the late actor John Barrymore, and the famous drummer, Gene Krupa, have their pets buried. At the other end of the scale, the largest American pet cemetery, which opened in 1972, is the 50-acre Bubbling Wells Pet Memorial Park in California, although this is predominantly taken up as a resting place for dogs.

As the pet cemetery in Hyde Park, London, fell into disuse long ago, pet-owners in the UK, in recent times, have been quick to make their wishes in regard to pet cemeteries known and, despite shortage of land, facilities are now available at a number of sites.

Perhaps the most recent are those offered by Silvermere Haven in Cobham, Surrey, which is located in peaceful country surroundings within easy reach of London, and also the Ipswich Pet Cemetery, where visitors are welcomed and plots can be marked by memorial stones or plaques.

Several veterinary surgeons now offer cremation facilities, while the Raystede Centre for Animal Welfare in Ringmer, Sussex, has a crematorium and peaceful garden of remembrance. The Jerry Green Foundation Trust in Broughton, Brigg, Lincolnshire, has a cemetery and a garden of rest.

There is also an animal cemetery at the People's Dispensary for Sick Animals sanitorium in Ilford, Essex, where a number of famous animals are buried, but this is closed now unless an owner already has a grave in which there is room for a further pet.

What I find particularly appealing about the facilities of the Jerry Green Foundation Trust is the scheme whereby owners who feel that they might predecease their pets can will them to the Trust. Such animals either live out their natural lives at one of the Trust's sanctuaries or are found a good home under the supervision of a welfare visiting scheme. When they die they will be buried in the Garden of Rest and their memory perpetuated by an inscribed plaque placed on their grave.

These are only a few of the burial facilities which exist for animals and, although they by no means represent every area, you will find that most animal welfare societies have an up-to-date record of those best known.

You may think that money spent in commemorating the life of an animal is wasteful but it is up to the individual to measure the worth of the love and devotion given to them by their pet and to take whatever action they think fit.

Before concluding this chapter I must, at the risk of sounding morbid, remind readers that we, like our pets, are not immortal, and that it is extremely important to make arrangements for them in the event of our predeceasing them. This is a problem which is unlikely to arise when one is part of a large, animal-loving family but it must never be overlooked in the case of a pet-owner living alone. I recently received a letter from a widowed lady wanting advice on the purchase of a pet and asking whether I thought she was now too old to own one.

The advice that I gave would have applied whether she was 30 or 70 years old. This was to go ahead, purchase the pet and enjoy it, but to be sure to make arrangements for its care should anything happen to her, making sure that such wishes were clearly written down and made known to a neighbour and her legal adviser.

10
Feline societies

Many people feel, having purchased a cat, that they would like to join or help a cat welfare society. To name all such worthwhile organisations in a book of this size would be impossible. However, I will deal with a few, all of which would be glad of your support.

Several of the major societies have branches in individual areas with which they will happily put enquirers in touch, while those societies I have not mentioned should be located easily at any good reference library.

Best known in the UK is the Royal Society for the Prevention of Cruelty to Animals (RSPCA) with headquarters at Horsham in Sussex and branches throughout the country; it has rescue kennels, hospitals, a network of inspectors and, of course, is under Royal patronage.

Only fractionally less well-known is the People's Dispensary for Sick Animals. The PDSA was formed in 1917 and, each year, provides free treatment for nearly one million animals belonging to people unable to afford private veterinary fees. The Society has over sixty animal treatment centres in the UK and overseas and is supported entirely by voluntary contributions.

Similar facilities exist in the USA. As might be expected, when one realises that as many as 10 000 cats and dogs are born every hour in the USA, there are numerous organisations endeavouring to do their best for them. Indeed, if one quotes from a leaflet issued by the American Society for the Prevention of Cruelty to Animals (ASPCA): 'Even if each family took in one of these animals, every American home would be filled within three years'.

The ASPCA was chartered in 1866 by a special act of the New York State legislature. It was the first, and today is still the largest, private humane society in the USA and is a leader in the humane movement of that country.

The work or the ASPCA brings it into direct contact with more than 200 000 animals each year; its clinic treats 20 000, the Animalport at John F. Kennedy International Airport handles 50 000. Approximately 16 000 animals a year are adopted from ASPCA shelters and, apart from these statistics, its underlying goals and principles are broad and highly commendable both in scope and in impact.

Equally commendable is the American Humane Association, based in Colorado, a tax-exempt organisation, formed in 1877 and incorporated into Washington DC in 1903. It is a federation of agencies throughout the USA and Canada, dedicated to the prevention of cruelty to both children and animals. It advises enquirers on how to become actively involved with animals in their community, whether by writing to officials or joining local branches and societies, offers a wide selection of educational material and coordinates a wide variety of programmes and services for individuals of all ages.

There is also, of course, the Bide-A-Wee Home Association, the first branch of which was established in New York City in 1903 by humanitarian, Flora D'Auby Jenkins Kibbe, who began the first Bide-A-Wee home as a shelter and adoption agency for homeless animals. Mrs Kibbe and a small volunteer staff set new standards for humane treatment of unwanted cats, dogs and other friendless animals.

Today, Bide-A-Wee is one of the largest private organisations of its kind in the USA and one of the most respected. Its advice and counsel on humane activities is constantly being sought, and the same principle upon which Mrs Kibbe founded the organisation still endures—an animal is never destroyed unless it is so ill that it stands no chance of recovering.

Not surprisingly, well-known actors and writers are often pet-owners, perhaps because their hours of work are flexible and they have more time to look after animals. Certainly a large number of celebrities are great animal-lovers, so it is no surprise to find the famous associated with and working for animal welfare. David Jacobs, for instance, the well-known radio and television personality, is a committee member of the Royal Society for the Prevention of

Cruelty to Animals in the UK and Katie Boyle works tirelessly for a number of animal charities.

In the USA, show business people run their own welfare society under the name of 'Actors and Others for Animals'. Those actively involved include Paul Newman and his wife, Joanne Woodward, Fred McMurray and his wife, former actress June Haver, Burt Reynolds, Zsa Zsa Gabor, Doris Day and many others. While most of the organisations mentioned cater for all domestic pets, there are also those which cater exclusively for the cat, such as Pet Pride, the national humane society for cats in California and the National Cat Protection Society, also in California, and the Save a Cat League based in New York.

In the UK, one extremely active body is the Cats Protection League, founded in 1927. This is the oldest charity devoted solely to the welfare of cats, its object being to rescue and rehabilitate strays, unwanted and injured cats, and to find homes for them where possible, to provide information to the public on the care of cats and kittens and, needless to say, to encourage the neutering of all those cats not required for breeding.

Somewhat more specialised is the work of the Cat Action Trust, which helps with the problems of Feral cats. The Trust captures those cats that live in wild communities and neuters them. It then either finds homes for them or returns them to the places where they were captured.

On a more technical level, but certainly invaluable, is the work of the Feline Advisory Bureau, known as FAB, which was formed by Joan Judd in 1958. Its two main objects are to promote humane behaviour towards the cat and to ensure its physical and mental well-being by advising owners on care in both health and sickness. It also establishes such special funds as may be thought desirable to promote investigation into feline diseases. Indeed, by joining FAB, members are helping current studies into all diseases, many aspects of which baffle and defeat diagnosis and treatment and still remain a mystery to owners and veterinary surgeons alike.

And, in conclusion, there is the Cat Survival Trust which works for the conservation of wild cats with particular emphasis on the smaller and less well-known species. It also seeks to advance public knowledge of wild cats and to conduct behavioural research in conjunction with university and other educational institutions.

So you see there are many, many people working for feline welfare in the UK and the USA and, indeed, all over the world. A list of the organisations mentioned and many others will be found on page 89. If you would like to become involved with any one of them your offer will be warmly accepted.

Useful addresses

United Kingdom

The Blue Cross (animal hospital), 1 Hugh Street, London SW1D 1QQ.
British Small Animals Veterinary Association, c/o Bell's Cottage, Gracious Street, Selbourne, Alton, Hampshire.
British Veterinary Association, 7 Mansfield Street, London W1M 0AT.
Catac Products Ltd (cat accessories), 1 Newham Street, Newham, Bedford, Bedfordshire.
Cat Action Trust, c/o The Crippetts, Jordans, Beaconsfield, Buckinghamshire.
Cat Survival Trust, Marlind Centre, Codicote Road, Welling, Hertfordshire AL6 9TU.
Cats Protection League, 20 North Street, Horsham, West Sussex.
Central Dog Registry (tattoos), 49 Marloes Road, London W8.
Feline Advisory Bureau (FAB), c/o Bell's Cottage, Gracious Street, Selbourne, Alton, Hampshire.
Anthony Green and Co. (*Pets Bazaar*), Kilburn Place, London NW6 4LZ.
Jerry Green Foundation Trust, Broughton, Brigg, Lincolnshire.
Governing Council of the Cat Fancy, Dovefields, Petworth Road, Witley, Surrey.
Harrods, Knightsbridge, London SW1.
Ipswich Pet Cemetery, 52 Brooklands Road, Brantham, Manningtree, Essex.
National Cat Club, The Laurels, Chesham Lane, Wendover, Buckinghamshire.
Pedigree Education Centre, Melton Mowbray, Leicestershire LE13 1BP.
Pet Plan Limited (cat insurance), 35 Horn Lane, London W3 9TA.
People's Dispensary for Sick Animals (sanitorium), Woodford Bridge Road, Ilford, Essex.

USEFUL ADDRESSES

People's Dispensary for Sick Animals, PDSA House, South Street, Dorking, Surrey.
Raystede Centre for Animal Welfare, Ringmer, Sussex.
Royal Society for the Prevention of Cruelty to Animals, Causeway, Horsham, Sussex RH12 1HG.
Silvermere Haven (pet cemetery), Byfleet Road, Cobham, Surrey.
Spillers Pet Advisory Service, New Malden House, 1 Blagdon Road, New Malden, Surrey KT3 4TB.

United States of America

Actors and Others for Animals, Beverley Hills, California.
American Cat Fanciers Association, PO Box 203, Point Lookout, Missouri 65726.
American Feline Society, 41 Union Square West, New York, NY 10003.
American Humane Association, 5351 South Roslyn Street, Englewood, Colorado 8011.
American Society for the Prevention of Cruelty to Animals (ASPCA), 441 East 92nd Street, New York, NY 10028.
Animal Protection Institute of America, 5694 South Land Park Drive, PO Box 22505, Sacramento, California 95822.
Bide-A-Wee Home Association, 410 East 38th Street, New York, NY 10016.
Bide-A-Wee Memorial Parks (see above).
Bubbling Wells Pet Memorial Park, California. (Address not available.)
Cat Book Center, Box 112 Wyka Station, New Rochelle, New York, NY 10804.
Cat Fanciers Federation, 2013 Elizabeth Street, Schenectady, New York, NY 12303.
I. D. Pet Service Center, PO Box 2244, Noroton Heights, Connecticut 06820.
Independent Cat Association, Suite 201, 211 East Olive, Burbank, California 91502.
Macy's Department Store, Herald Square, Broadway at 34th Street, New York, NY 10001.
National Cat Protection Society, 340 West Willow, Long Beach, California 90806.
Pet Pride (national humane society for cats), 15113 Sunset Boulevard, Pacific Palisades, California 90272.
Save a Cat League, 245 West 25th Street, New York, NY 10001.

References

Books

Cutts and Payne (1981) *Pedigree cats and kittens: how to choose and care for them* Batsford (B.T. Ltd), London.
Dale-Smith, P. (1963) *The cult of the cat* Heinemann Ltd, London.
Dunnil, M. (1974) *The Siamese cat owner's encyclopedia* Pelham Books Ltd, London.
Fox, M. (1974) *Understanding your cat* Blond & Briggs Ltd, London.
Henrie, M. (1980) *Cats* Franklin Watts Ltd, London
Johnson, N. H. and Galin, S. (1980) *The complete cat and kitten book* Hale (Robert) Ltd, London.
Palmer, J. (1980) *Cats and kittens* Ward Lock Ltd, London.
Pond, G., editor (1972) *Complete cat encyclopaedia* Heinemann Ltd, London.
Pond, G. (1979) *The observer's book of cats* Warne (Frederick) (Publishers) Ltd, London.
Pond, G. (1982) *The cat* Orbis, London.
Richards, D.S. (1977) *Handbook of pedigree cat breeding* Batsford (B.T. Ltd), London.
Richards, D.S. (1981) *A cat of your own* Salamander Books Ltd, London.
Richards, D.S. (1982) *Illustrated guide to cats* Salamander Books Ltd, London.
Taylor, D. (1980) *The cat* Unwin Brothers Ltd, Surrey.
West, G. (1981) *All about your cat's health* Pelham Books Ltd, London.
Wright, M. and Walters, S. editors (1980) *The big book of the cat* Ward Lock Ltd, London.

Periodicals

All Cats (Monthly. c/o Pet Pride, 15113 Sunset, Pacific, Palisades, California 90272.)

Cats (Monthly. c/o Watmoughs Ltd, Idle, Bradford, Yorkshire.)
Cats World Monthly (c/o Scan House, Southwick Street, Brighton BN4 4TE.)
Cats and Catdom Annual (c/o Watmoughs Ltd, Idle, Bradford, Yorkshire.)
The Pets Welcome Holiday Guide (Annually. c/o Herald Advisory Services, 234 Brighton Road, South Croydon, Surrey CR2 6OE.)

Index

Numbers in *italics* refer to illustrations.

Abandoned animals 71
Abscesses 76
Abyssinian 26-7
  Lilac *26*
Abyssinian Cat Club 27
Accessories 43-4
Accidents 71, 73, 76
Accommodation 14, 67
Actors and Others for Animals 87
American Humane Association 86
American Society for the Prevention of Cruelty to Animals 37, 85-6
Anal glands 77
Angora 16, 17, 31
  Chocolate *31*
Animal Protection Institute of America 37
Animals Act of 1971 71
Anti-cruelty laws 71
Associations 85-8
Awards 59-62

Balinese 17, 21
  Blue-point *21*

Basket *39*, 39-40, 43
Bathing *60*, 77
Bedding 40, 43, 67
Behaviour 7, 9
Bide-a-Wee Association 37, 81-2, 86
Birman 17, 33
  Seal-point *33*
Black cat 29
Bladder stones 77
Breed
  classes 59-62
  numbers 16, 17-18, 19, 59
  standards 15, 16, 19, 29, 54, 59
Breeding 9, 13, 36, 37, 65-9
  quarters *52*
Bubbling Wells Pet Memorial Park 81-2
Burial facilities 83
Burmese 22, 27, 33, 36
  Blue *22*
  Cream *49*
Burns 76

Canadian Cat Association 56
Care 12, 14, 49-52
Carrying basket *42*, *42*
Cat Action Trust 87

Cat Club 55
Cat Fanciers Association Inc. 15, 38, 55, 56, 57-8
Cat Fanciers Federation Inc. 38, 56
Cat Fancy 13, 15, 38, 53-4, 55
Cat fever *see* Infectious feline enteritis
Cat flap 13, 14, 41, *41*, 50
Cat flu 74, 75
Cat Survival Trust 87
Cat worship 10
Cattery 51, 66, 74
Cats Protection League 37, 87
Cemeteries 81-4
Championships 59-62
Characteristics of cats 11-12
Cheetah 7, 9
Chinchilla 30
   White *30*
Climbing-tree 43
Collar 42, *42*, 43, 44, 72
   flea 78
Congenital deafness 32
Conservation 87
Constipation 77
Cremation 83

Diarrhoea 78
Digestive complaints 77
Diseases 74-9
Distemper 75
Dishes 39, *39*, 43
Domestication 10-11

Ear mites 78
Egyptians 10, 11, 23, 26
Elizabethan collar *76*
Euthanasia 37, 78, 81
Exercise 13, 14, 50
   Siamese 21

Fecundity 37, 65
Feeding 14, 45-8
   adults 45-7
   kittens 47-8, 68-9
   pregnant queens 66-7
Feline Advisory Bureau 87
Feral cat 9, 10, 36, 87
Food
   canned 45, 46, 48, 68
   calorific values 46-7

Geoffroy's cat *8*, 9
Grass 39, 77
Grooming 41, *60*, *61*, 76
   equipment *41*

Hairballs 77, 79
Hairless cat 23, 35-6
Halitosis 78
Harness 43
Havana *28*, 28-9
Heater 40
Hereditary faults 65
Holdalls 43
Holidays 51
Himalayan 17
Hygiene 40, 50

Identification 42-3, 72
   capsule *42*
Infectious feline enteritis 51, 75
Inoculations 51, 74-5
Insecticides 78
Insurance 51, 74
Introduction to Britain
   domestic cat 10
   Korat 27-8
   Russian Blue 26
Ipswich Pet Cemetery 83

Japanese Bobtail 35
Jerry Green Foundation Trust 83
Judges 56, 58, 62, *63*, 63-4

Kidney stones 77
Kittening 67-8
Kittening box 67, *67*

INDEX

Kittens 13, 37, 50, *50*, 64, 67-8, *68*, 74, 76
Korat *27*, 27-8, 29

Laws 71-2, 81
Laxatives 77
Litter size 67-8
Litter tray 41, *49*, 49-50
Long-hairs 16, 17-18, 41, 59
    Bicolour *15*
    Black 29, *29*
    Blue *60*, *61*
    Cream *63*
    Self Red *58*
    White 32, *32*
Longevity 73, 81
Lost animals 50, 72

Magic 10, 11, 29
Maine Coon cat 36
Manx 34
    Black *34*
Mating 66
Mortality 75
Mutation 23, 24, 36

National Cat Club 55
National Cat Protection Society 87
Neutering 37, 52, 87
Newspaper 67

Organisations 37, 38, 54-5, 56-8, 89-90
Origins
    Angora 31, 32
    Birman 33
    domestic cat 7, 9
    Korat 28
    Long-hairs 16, 17
    Russian Blue 25
    Short-hairs 16
    Siamese 19
Ownership, responsibilities 13-14, 71

Pallas, Peter Simon 19
Panleukopenia *see* Infectious feline enteritis
Parasites 78
Pedigree cats 14-15, 37, 53, 55
People's Dispensary for Sick Animals 37, 74, 83, 85
Persians 17, 21, 31, 36
    Peke-faced 35
Pet classes 59-60
Pet Pride 87
Pill administration 79
Playthings 50, *50*
Pneumonitis 75-6
Pregnancy 66-7
Publications 57
Purchasing a cat 36-8

Quarantine 71-2
Queen Victoria 11, 55

Ragdoll 36
Raystede Centre for Animal Welfare 83
Recuperative powers 73
Respiratory trouble 35
Rex 16, 23-24
    Cornish 14, *23*, 23-4
    Devon 23-4, *24*
Righting reflex 7
Road accidents 71, 73, 76
Rodent control 10, 11, 47
Routine 50-51
Royal Society for the Prevention of Cruelty to Animals 37, 42, 85, 87
Russian Blue 14, *25*, 25-6

Scalds 76
Scottish Fold 35
Scratching posts 40, *40*, 50
Season 66
Shampoo 77
Short-hairs 16, 18, 59
    British 16, *16*

Short-hairs—*cont.*
  Foreign 16, *17*, 18
Show cats, characteristics 53
Show pen *62*
Show world 53-64
Shows 53-4, 55, 56, 57, 58, 59-62
  Empire Cat Club 15, 38
  National Cat Club 15, 38, *54*, 55
Siamese 14, 16, 18, 19-21, 27, 28,
  29, 36, 59, 73
  Chocolate-point *20*
  Lilac-point *68*
Siamese Cat Club 55
Silvermere Haven 83
Sphynx 35-6
Stewarding 64
Studs 66

Tabby
  non-pedigree *9*
  Oriental *46*
  Silver *16*
Teeth 78

Temperature 39, 40, 50-51, 77
Ticks 78
Tiger *8*
Toilet facilities 41
Training 49-52
Transport 42, 46, 76
Turkish Van 17

Varieties of cat
  common 16-34
  unusual 35-6
Veterinary
  appointments 73
  fees 51, 74
Viral rhinotracheitis 76
Vocalisation 20
Vomiting 79

Weaning 68-9
White Long-hair, Odd-Eyed 32, *32*
Wild cats 7-9, 36
Worms 77, 79